Alan Jeffery

REVISE EDEXCEL GCSE Science

Additional Science

REVISION GUIDE

Foundation

Series Consultant: Harry Smith
Series Editor: Penny Johnson

Authors: Penny Johnson, Sue Kearsey, Damian Riddle

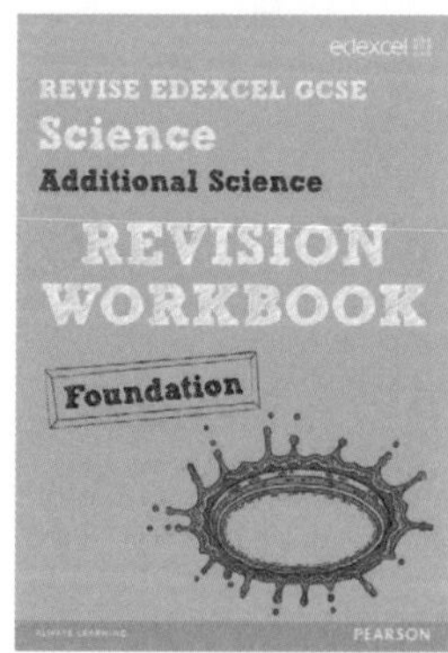

THE REVISE EDEXCEL SERIES

Available in print or online

Online editions for all titles in the Revise Edexcel series are available Autumn 2012.

Presented on our ActiveLearn platform, you can view the full book and customise it by adding notes, comments and weblinks.

Print editions

Additional Science Revision Guide Foundation 9781446902639

Additional Science Revision Workbook Foundation 9781446902646

Online editions

Additional Science Revision Guide Foundation 9781446904534

Additional Science Revision Workbook Foundation 9781446904541

Print and online editions are also available for Science (Higher and Foundation), Additional Science (Higher) and Extension Units.

This Revision Guide is designed to complement your classroom and home learning, and to help prepare you for the exam. It does not include all the content and skills needed for the complete course. It is designed to work in combination with Edexcel's main GCSE Science 2011 Series.

To find out more visit:
www.pearsonschools.co.uk/edexcelgcsesciencerevision

ALWAYS LEARNING PEARSON

Contents

1-to-1 page match with the Foundn Revision Workbook
ISBN 9781446902646

A small bit of small print

Target grade ranges are quoted in this book for some of the questions. Students targeting this grade range should be aiming to get most of the marks available. Students targeting a higher grade should be aiming to get all of the marks available.

Edexcel publishes Sample Assessment Material and the Specification on its website. This is the official content and this book should be used in conjunction with it. The questions in *Now try this* have been written to help you practise every topic in the book. Remember: the real exam questions may not look like this.

Plant and animal cells

Animals and plants are formed from cells. Animal cells and plant cells have some parts in common. These parts have particular functions in a cell.

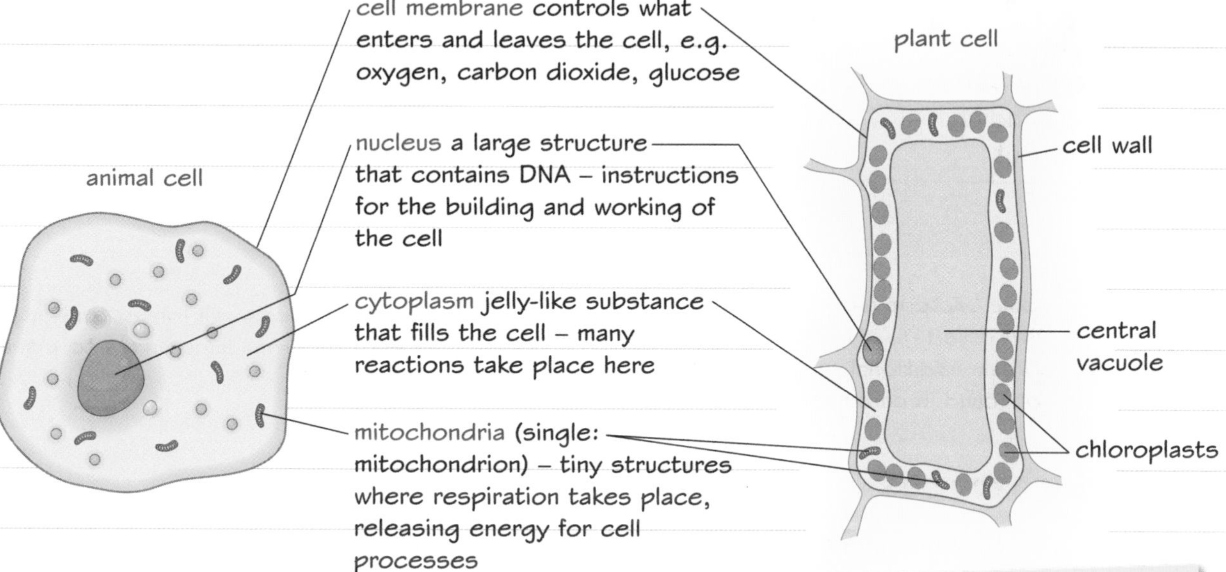
animal cell
plant cell
cell membrane controls what enters and leaves the cell, e.g. oxygen, carbon dioxide, glucose
nucleus a large structure that contains DNA – instructions for the building and working of the cell
cytoplasm jelly-like substance that fills the cell – many reactions take place here
mitochondria (single: mitochondrion) – tiny structures where respiration takes place, releasing energy for cell processes
cell wall
central vacuole
chloroplasts

The cytoplasm of a cell is not a proper structure, such as a membrane or chloroplast. It is the jelly-like substance that fills the cell and supports other structures.

Worked example

Name the three structures that are found in most plant cells but not animal cells, and describe their functions.

Chloroplasts are the structures where photosynthesis takes place to make food for the plant cell.

The cell wall is made of cellulose, and is tough so that it helps support the cell and helps it keep its shape.

The large central vacuole contains cell sap, which helps to keep the plant cell rigid.

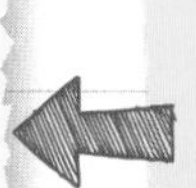

Watch out! The cell membrane and cell wall are different and separate structures.

Now try this

target G-C

1. Draw up a table like the one below to show the parts of plant and animal cells. Complete the table to show the following: cell wall, cell membrane, chloroplasts, cytoplasm, mitochondria, nucleus, vacuole.

Component	Found in plant cells?	Found in animal cells?	Function

(7 marks)

target F-C

2. Explain why chloroplasts are only found in plant cells. **(2 marks)**
3. Explain which parts of a plant cell help plants to support themselves. **(2 marks)**

Inside bacteria

Bacterial cells

Bacteria have a simple cell structure. Like animal and plant cells, they have a cell membrane surrounding the cytoplasm. But they do not have a nucleus.

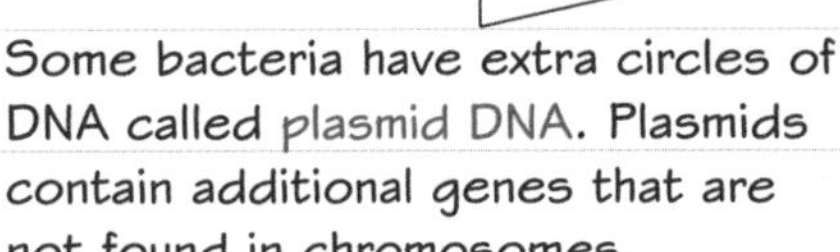

A single loop of chromosomal DNA lies free in the cytoplasm. This carries most of the bacterial genes.
cell membrane
Some bacteria have a flagellum to help them move.
Some bacteria have extra circles of DNA called plasmid DNA. Plasmids contain additional genes that are not found in chromosomes.
Many bacteria have a cell wall for protection, but it is made of different substances to plant cell walls.

Using microscopes

Before microscopes were invented about 350 years ago, we could not see the cells in organisms. Magnification enables us to see plant cells, animal cells and bacterial cells, and the structures inside them.

A light microscope uses light to magnify objects. The greatest possible magnification using a light microscope is about ×2000.

An electron microscope uses electrons to view an object. This makes it possible to magnify objects up to about ×10 million. We can see far more detail in cells with an electron microscope than with a light microscope.

Worked example

Some cells were viewed by microscope using a ×4 eyepiece and ×20 objective. Calculate the magnification of the cells seen through the microscope.

magnification of object

$$= \text{magnification of eyepiece} \times \text{magnification of objective}$$

$$= 4 \times 20 = 80$$

The cells will be magnified 80 times by the microscope.

EXAM ALERT!

Always show your working in a calculation. Even if you get the final answer wrong you may be able to show that you understand steps in the calculation.

Students have struggled with exam questions similar to this - **be prepared!** ResultsPlus

Now try this

1. **(a)** Name two structures seen in bacterial cells that are not seen in a plant cell. **(2 marks)**
   (b) Name one structure seen in an animal cell that is not seen in a bacterial cell. **(1 mark)**
2. A plant cell that is 0.05 mm long is viewed under a light microscope. The objective is ×40 and the eyepiece is ×5. Calculate the size of the image of the cell. **(2 marks)**

DNA

Extracting DNA

DNA can be extracted from cells using detergent, salt, a protease enzyme and ice-cold ethanol.

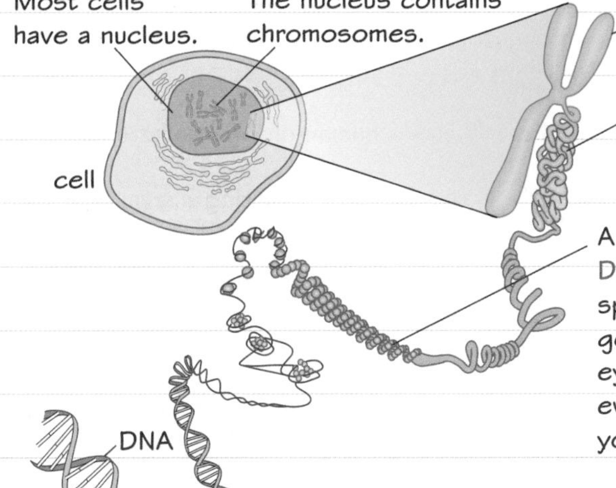

Most cells have a nucleus.
The nucleus contains chromosomes.
cell
chromosome
A chromosome consists of a string of genes.
A gene is a short piece of DNA that codes for a specific protein. You have genes for hair structure, eye colour, enzymes and every other protein in your body.
DNA
Each gene is a length of DNA. DNA is a long, coiled molecule formed from two strands. The strands are twisted in a double helix.
G C
A T
C G
A T
T A
The two strands of the double helix are joined by pairs of bases. There are four different bases in DNA:
A = adenine T = thymine
C = cytosine G = guanine
Bases form complementary pairs:
A always pairs with T
C always pairs with G.
Weak hydrogen bonds between the base pairs hold the DNA strands together.

EXAM ALERT!

Only a quarter of students got full marks on a recent question about DNA. When answering exam questions on DNA remember that the two strands in DNA are held together by weak hydrogen bonds between the complementary base pairs.

Students have struggled with this topic in recent exams - **be prepared!** ResultsPlus

Remember: straight A with straight T; curly C with curly G.

Worked example

Describe the roles of Maurice Wilkins, Rosalind Franklin, James Watson and Francis Crick in the discovery of the structure of DNA.

Maurice Wilkins and Rosalind Franklin studied DNA structure using X-rays. Franklin used photographs of DNA to work out how the atoms were grouped.

James Watson and Francis Crick used data from other scientists to help them work out the structure of DNA. Franklin's photographs gave them the final clue to help them build their double helix model.

Now try this

1. Identify where genes are found in a cell. **(1 mark)**
2. Write a sentence to explain each of these words:
   (a) gene **(b)** DNA **(c)** base. **(3 marks)**

target E-C

3. The sequence of bases on one strand of DNA is CGAT. Write down the sequence of bases on the complementary strand, and explain how you worked out your answer. **(2 marks)**

Genetic engineering

In genetic engineering (also called genetic modification) a gene from one organism is inserted into the DNA of another organism. The inserted gene then makes its protein in the genetically modified (GM) organism.

1. A gene (e.g. for insulin) is cut out of a human chromosome using enzymes.

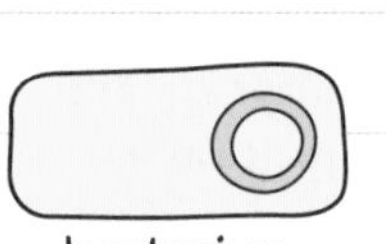

3. The human insulin gene and the plasmid are mixed together.

4. The human insulin gene and the plasmid are stuck together to make a new plasmid.

2. A DNA plasmid is taken out of a bacterium and cut open using enzymes.

5. The new plasmid with the human insulin gene is put back into a bacterium. The bacterium has been genetically modified. The bacterium will now make human insulin.

Advantages and disadvantages of genetic engineering

- ✓ Making human insulin using GM bacteria is quicker and cheaper than producing it any other way. So more people with diabetes can be treated.
- ✗ A few diabetic people react badly to this insulin and need a different form.
- ✓ 'Golden rice' is a GM plant that contains genes from other plants for a protein that makes vitamin A in the human body. It could prevent illness due to lack of vitamin A in people who mainly eat rice.
- ✗ Golden rice seed costs more than normal rice seed, so the poorest people can't afford to grow it.

Worked example

Crop plants can be genetically modified with a gene that protects them from being killed by a herbicide. Describe some advantages and disadvantages of growing GM crops.

Advantages: Only the weed plants will die, so the crop plants will have more room to grow. This should increase the crop yield.

Disadvantages: If the gene for herbicide resistance passes to weed plants, the weeds will no longer be killed by the herbicide. So the cost of making GM crop plants will be wasted. Also, overuse of herbicides can reduce biodiversity.

Now try this

1. (a) Name the type of organism that is genetically modified to produce human insulin. **(1 mark)**
   (b) Explain why this genetically modified organism produces the human form of insulin. **(1 mark)**
2. Explain what we mean by a genetically modified organism. **(2 marks)**
3. Describe how an organism could be genetically modified to produce a new characteristic. **(3 marks)**

Mitosis

There are two types of cell division. Mitosis is the cell division that happens in body cells. A body cell is any cell except those that produce gametes (sex cells).

Three things to remember
- Mi-TWO-sis makes TWO cells
- MiTosis makes idenTical cells
- Diploid means double (two sets of) chromosomes

The cell that divides is called the parent cell. → The parent cell divides to form two daughter cells.

The parent cell is a diploid cell. This means it has two sets of chromosomes.

Before the parent cell divides, each chromosome is copied exactly.

When the cell divides in two, each cell gets one copy of each chromosome.

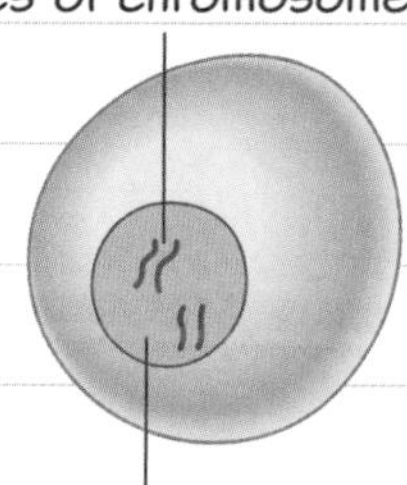

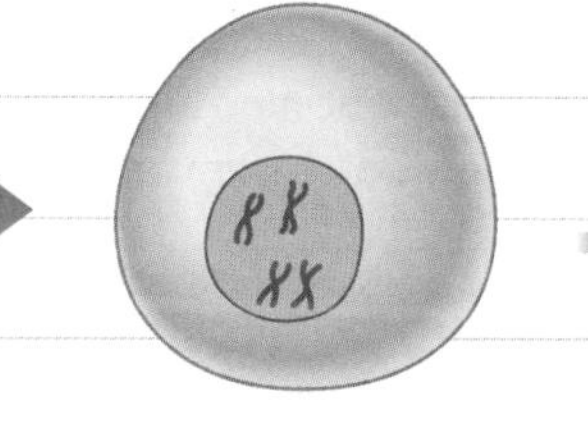

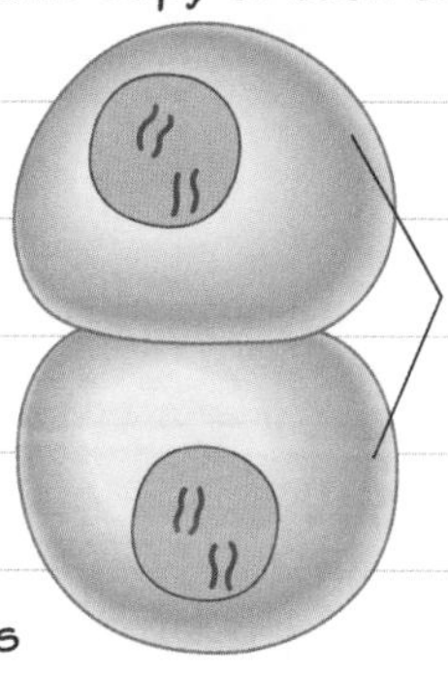

The daughter cells are genetically identical. They are also diploid cells.

nucleus

The chromosomes are drawn short here, and coloured, so it is easier to see what is happening. They don't really look like this.

Worked example

Name three situations where mitosis is used to produce new cells.

Mitosis produces new body cells for:
- growth
- repairing damaged parts of the body
- asexual reproduction.

Remember: asexual reproduction produces genetically identical offspring.

Asexual reproduction

Asexual reproduction is the production of new organisms without fertilisation, such as when:
- bacteria split in two to make more bacteria
- plants make new plantlets that split off from the parent plant to grow on their own.

Now try this

target G-D

1. In mitosis:
   (a) State how many daughter cells are produced from each parent cell. **(1 mark)**
   (b) State whether the daughter cells are genetically different or identical to the parent cell. **(1 mark)**

target G-E

2. Give two examples of asexual reproduction. **(2 marks)**

target E-C

3. Explain how body cells are genetically identical diploid cells. **(2 marks)**

Fertilisation and meiosis

Fertilisation takes place during sexual reproduction. Fertilisation is when a male gamete (sex cell) combines with a female gamete to produce a zygote.

Gametes are haploid cells. They have only one set of chromosomes. → The zygote has two sets of chromosomes. So it is a diploid cell.

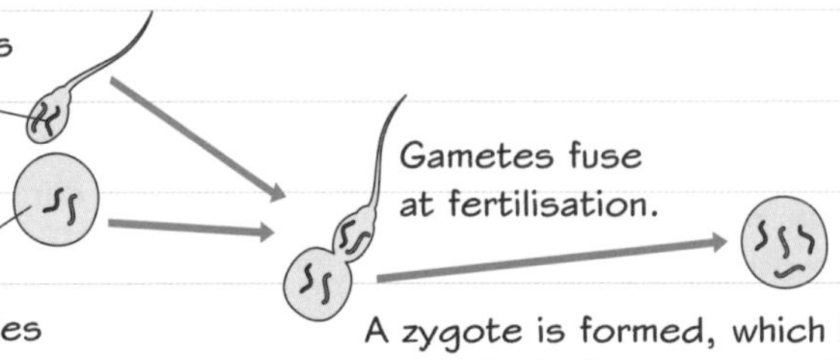

Sperm cell (gamete) carries chromosomes from the father.

Egg cell (gamete) carries chromosomes from the mother.

Gametes fuse at fertilisation.

A zygote is formed, which has one set of chromosomes from the mother and one set from the father.

Remember: sexual reproduction produces variation in the offspring. Asexual reproduction produces offspring that are genetically identical.

Meiosis

Meiosis is the second type of cell division. It happens when a diploid cell divides to produce haploid gametes (sex cells, such as sperm and egg cells).

Remember: haploid cells, produced by meiosis (me-1-osis), have 1 set of chromosomes.

The parent cell is a diploid cell. So it has two sets of chromosomes. → The parent cell divides in two and then in two again. Four daughter cells are produced.

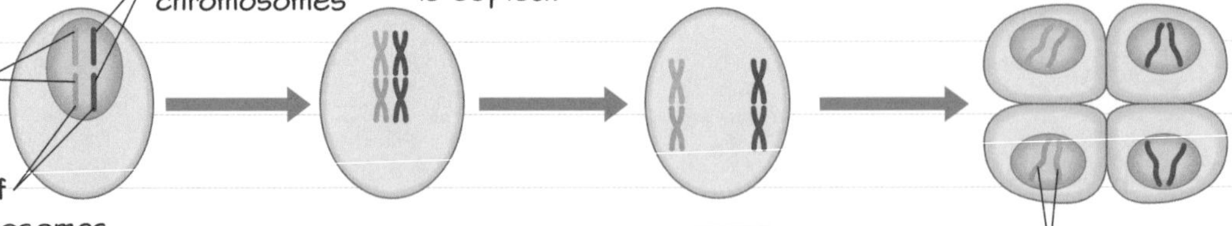

one set of chromosomes

the other set of chromosomes

pair of chromosomes

Before the parent cell divides, each chromosome is copied.

Each daughter cell gets a copy of one chromsome from each pair.

Each daughter cell has only one set of chromosomes. So these are haploid cells.

The cells produced by division are always called 'daughter cells' even if they will eventually turn into sperm cells.

Now try this

target G-D

1. In meiosis:
   (a) State the number of daughter cells formed from one parent cell. **(1 mark)**
   (b) State how many sets of chromosomes each gamete has. **(1 mark)**

target E-C

2. Describe the process of fertilisation, using the words diploid, gamete, haploid and zygote in your answer. **(4 marks)**

Making clones

A clone is an organism that has the same genes as another organism. Cloning is an example of asexual reproduction.

sexual reproduction

Sexual reproduction produces offspring that show variation.

Cloning produces offspring that are identical.

Plants can be cloned by taking cuttings.

Cloning mammals

We can clone mammals to produce new organisms that are genetically identical.

- ✓ If the animal has useful features all of its offspring will have the same good features.
- ✗ It is more difficult to clone a mammal than a plant. It may take many attempts before a healthy cloned mammal is born, and each attempt costs more money.
- ✗ Cloned mammals may suffer more health problems than usual, which may cause them to die early.

Worked example

A farmer has a prize bull. Other farmers buy sperm from her bull to fertilise their cows to produce high-quality calves. State one advantage and one disadvantage of cloning the prize bull.

Advantage: The farmer will have more bulls that produce sperm that other farmers want to buy, so she will get more money.

Disadvantage: If it takes too many attempts to clone the bull, the farmer may spend more money than she can gain from selling the sperm.

Now try this

target F-D

1. Write a definition for the term 'clone' in your own words. **(2 marks)**
2. Genetic modification is used to produce GM goats that have human hormones in their milk. The GM goats are then cloned to produce cloned goats.

target E-C

   (a) Will the cloned goats produce the human hormones or not? Explain your answer. **(2 marks)**
   (b) Describe one risk of producing more goats by cloning. **(1 mark)**

Stem cells

Cells in an embryo are unspecialised. They divide to produce all the differentiated cells in the body, such as neurones and muscle cells. Once the cells have differentiated they cannot divide to produce other kinds of cell. Stem cells are cells that can divide to produce many types of cell. There are embryonic stem cells and adult stem cells.

Worked example

Describe how embryonic stem cells change as an animal matures.

Embryonic stem cells can differentiate into almost any type of cell. As the animal matures, most cells lose this ability. Only a few adult stem cells remain that can differentiate into a small range of different types of cell.

Research using stem cells

Some diseases are caused by faulty cells, such as cystic fibrosis. Scientists are researching how to use stem cells to produce replacement healthy cells for treating these diseases.

embryonic stem cells

✓ easy to extract from embryo

✓ produce any type of cell

✗ embryo destroyed when cells removed – some people see this as murder

✗ body recognises the cells as 'different' and will reject them without use of drugs

all stem cells

✓ replace faulty cell with healthy cell, so person is well again

! may produce cancer cells instead of healthy cells

adult stem cells

✓ no embryo destroyed so not an ethical issue

✓ if taken from the person to be treated, will not cause rejection by the body

✗ difficult to find and extract from tissue

✗ produce only a few types of cell

✓ - Advantage ✗ - Disadvantage ! - Risk

Now try this

1. (a) State how a stem cell is different from a normal body cell. **(1 mark)**
   (b) Write the meaning of 'differentiated cell' in your own words. **(1 mark)**

target E-C

2. (a) State why embryonic stem cells could be more useful than adult stem cells to replace faulty cells. **(1 mark)**
   (b) Explain your answer to part **(a)**. **(1 mark)**

3. (a) Describe an ethical problem with researching treatment using embryonic stem cells. **(1 mark)**
   (b) Explain your answer to part **(a)**. **(1 mark)**

4. Explain why the risk of cancer may be increased with the use of stem cells. **(2 marks)**

Protein synthesis

Cells use DNA to make proteins. Proteins are sequences of amino acids joined together. The order of the bases in the DNA defines the order in which the amino acids are joined together. Every protein is formed from a specific number of amino acids in a particular order. So each section of DNA codes for a particular protein.

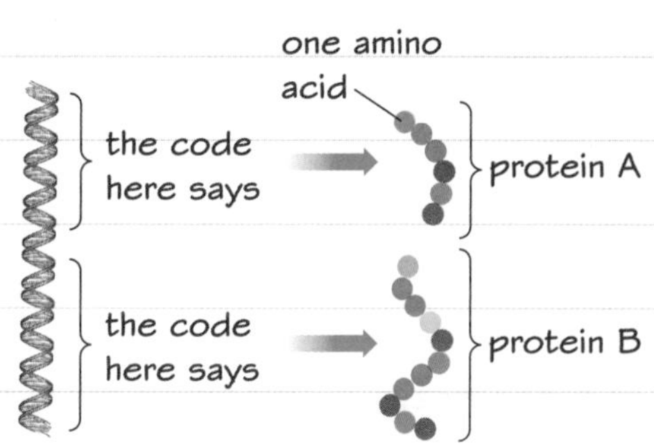

Different protein shapes

The order of amino acids gives each protein a particular 3D shape. The shape of a protein affects the way it works.

Shape	Examples	Functions
globular (blobby)	• enzymes	• control reactions due to their shape
	• hormones	• transported in blood to target cells
	• haemoglobin (in blood)	• carries oxygen in red blood cells
fibrous (long, strong fibres)	• keratin (in nails)	• tough nails protect finger and toe ends
	• collagen (in tendons and ligaments)	• ligaments hold bones together, tendons attach muscles to bones

Mutations

A mutation can change one or more of the bases in the DNA base sequence. This may change the protein that is produced from that section of DNA. This change may be harmful, beneficial or have no effect on the protein that the base sequence codes for. An example of a harmful mutation is the allele that causes sickle cell disease.

Worked example

Enzymes have a very specific shape that allows them to work effectively. Explain why a gene mutation can mean that an enzyme does not work so well.

A gene mutation can change the base sequence in DNA. If this change produces a different amino acid sequence, it may produce a different-shaped enzyme than before. Shape affects the way an enzyme functions, so a different shape will affect how well the enzyme works.

Now try this

1. Complete the sentence correctly.
   The sequence of .... in a DNA strand codes for a specific sequence of .... in a protein. **(2 marks)**
2. Define the term *mutation*. **(1 mark)**
3. Explain why different proteins have different shapes. **(2 marks)**

EXAM ALERT!

A recent exam asked a question on protein shape and around four out of five students gained no marks. Remember that the 3D shape of a protein is produced by the order of the amino acids in it.

Students have struggled with exam questions similar to this **- be prepared!** ResultsPlus

Enzymes

Enzymes are biological catalysts. Enzymes control reactions that take place in the body.

This means they are found in living organisms.

A catalyst changes the rate of a reaction but is not used up by the reaction.

Some of these enzyme-controlled reactions join substrate molecules together to make bigger product molecules. Other reactions break large molecules down into smaller molecules.

Enzymes inside cells

In DNA replication, the DNA strands are separated and two new strands are formed. Enzymes control each stage of the process.

One enzyme catalyses the splitting apart (unzipping) of the two DNA strands.

A different enzyme catalyses the joining together of bases to make new strands.

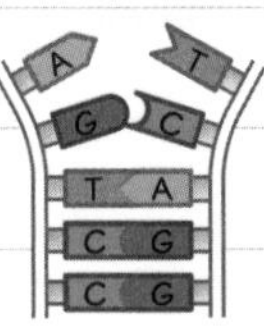

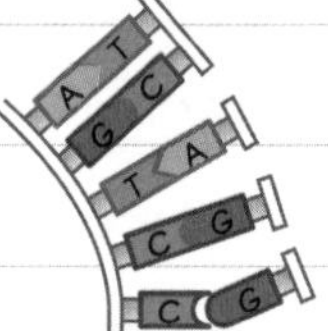

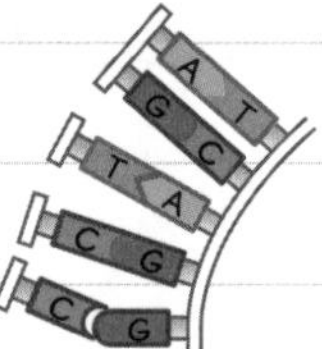

There are many reactions during protein synthesis, including building the new amino acid chain.

Each reaction in protein synthesis is controlled by a different enzyme.

Enzymes outside cells

Worked example

Explain why we release digestive enzymes into the gut from cells lining our digestive system.

The molecules in our food are too large to be absorbed into the body. Digestive enzymes break down these large molecules into much smaller ones. The small food molecules are small enough to be absorbed into our body, where they are used for growth and respiration.

Enzymes are not living organisms, but are substances found inside living organisms.

Now try this

1. Give one example of a process in the body where an enzyme breaks large molecules into smaller molecules. **(1 mark)**
2. Give one example of a process in the body where an enzyme builds larger molecules from small molecules. **(1 mark)**

target E-C

3. Explain why enzymes can be described as biological catalysts. **(2 marks)**

Enzyme action

The activity of an enzyme can be measured by measuring the rate of the reaction. The faster the reaction, the more active the enzyme. The activity of an enzyme can be affected by several factors.

Temperature

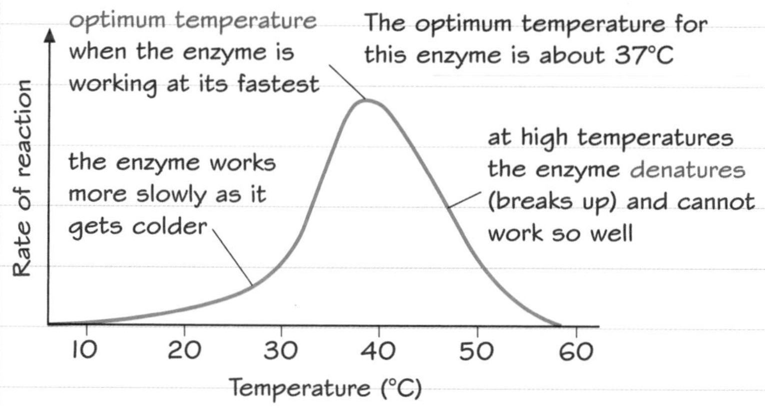
optimum temperature when the enzyme is working at its fastest
The optimum temperature for this enzyme is about 37°C
the enzyme works more slowly as it gets colder
at high temperatures the enzyme denatures (breaks up) and cannot work so well
Rate of reaction
10 20 30 40 50 60
Temperature (°C)

Substrate concentration

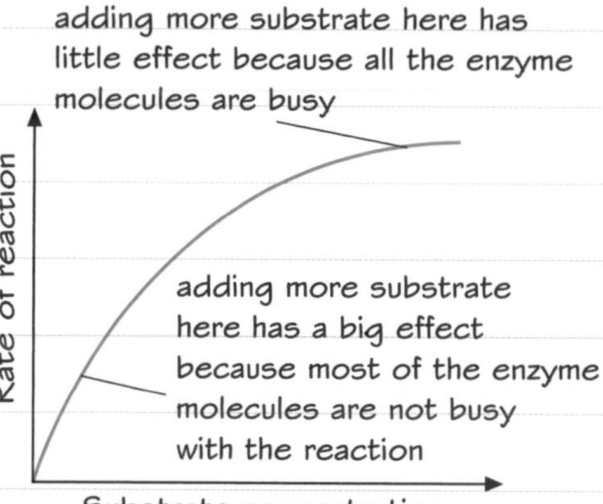
adding more substrate here has little effect because all the enzyme molecules are busy
Rate of reaction
adding more substrate here has a big effect because most of the enzyme molecules are not busy with the reaction
Substrate concentration

You can show the effect of changing a factor, such as pH, on enzyme activity by using an enzyme that breaks down an identifiable substance (e.g. starch) and measuring how quickly the substance is broken down under different conditions.

Worked example

The graph shows the rate of a reaction catalysed by an enzyme at different pHs. Use the graph to:

(a) identify the optimum pH for this enzyme

(b) help you explain what *optimum pH* means.

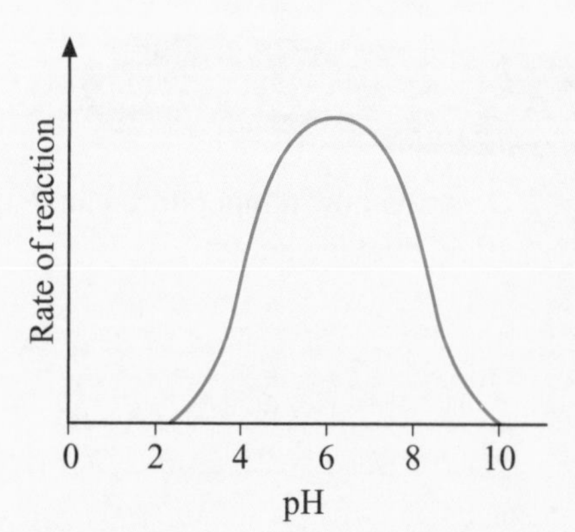
Rate of reaction
0 2 4 6 8 10
pH

(a) The optimum pH for this enzyme is about pH 6.

(b) The optimum pH is the point when the enzyme is working fastest, so the rate of reaction is at its highest point on the curve. When the pH is lower than this, or higher than this, the enzyme works more slowly so the rate of reaction is slower.

Now try this

target G-D
target F-C

1. Name three factors that can affect the activity of an enzyme. **(3 marks)**
2. Explain what the term optimum temperature means. **(1 mark)**
3. **(a)** One of the graphs above shows the effect of substrate concentration on rate of reaction. Describe what this graph shows. **(2 marks)**

   (b) Explain why the graph has this shape. **(2 marks)**

'Describe' means you should say what the graph looks like. 'Explain' means you should give a reason why the graph is this shape.

Explaining enzyme action

Enzyme molecules have a specific 3D shape. Part of this shape is the active site. This is where substrate molecules sit during a reaction. The shape of the substrate molecule and the shape of the active site must match for the reaction to take place.

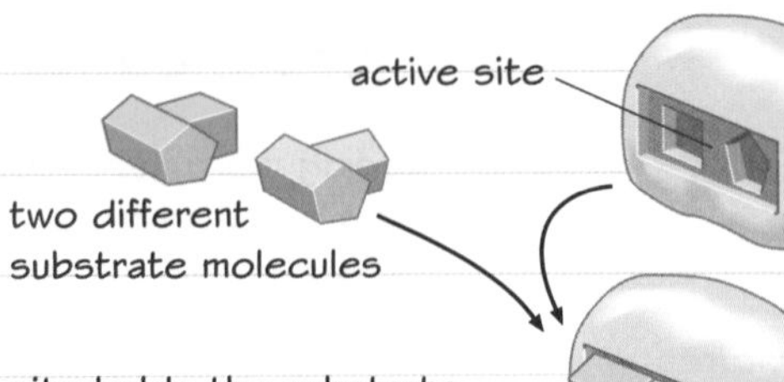

The product molecule is a slightly different shape to the substrate molecules. It doesn't fit the active site well, so it is released.

The active site holds the substrate molecules close together so they can join and form a product molecule.

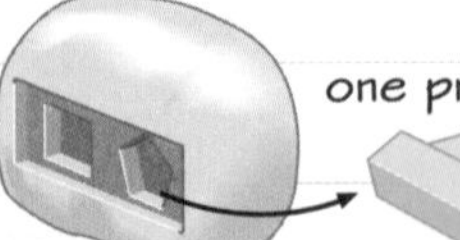

'Lock and key' hypothesis

The matching of the shape of the substrate with the shape of the active site is like choosing a key to open a lock. This is why the explanation of how an enzyme works is called the 'lock and key' hypothesis. This hypothesis helps explain why an enzyme is specific for a substrate (will only work with that substrate).

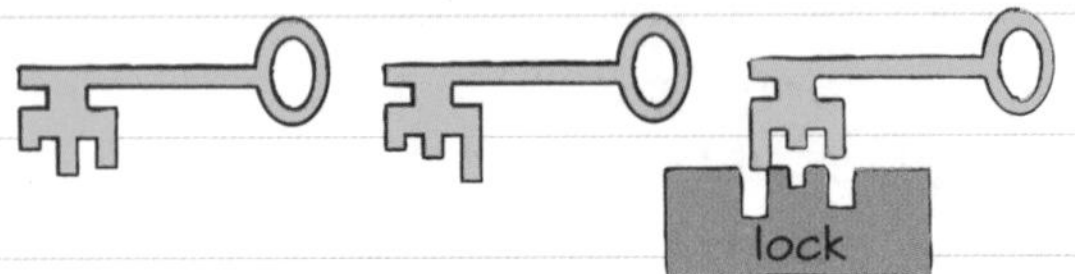

Only this key will fit and work in this lock.

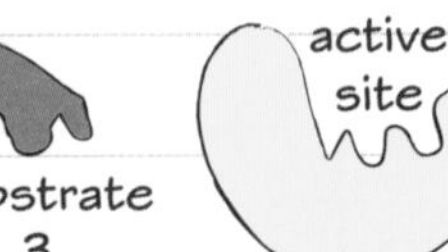

Only substrate 2 will fit and work in the active site of this enzyme.

Worked example

Extreme changes in pH can denature enzymes too.

Describe how temperature can denature an enzyme and so affect enzyme activity.

- High temperatures change the shape of enzymes.
- The shape of the active site is changed too.
- The substrate can't fit into the active site now.
- The enzyme is said to be denatured.
- The enzyme does not catalyse the reaction now.

EXAM ALERT!

Flowcharts, diagrams or bulleted lists can be used to answer questions as long as they include all the important information.

Students have struggled with exam questions similar to this - **be prepared!** ResultsPlus

Now try this

1. Complete the sentences.
   The space in an enzyme where the substrate fits is called the .... This is where the substrate is changed into the ....
   (2 marks)

2. Explain why an enzyme only works on one substrate. **(2 marks)**

3. Explain how the 'lock and key' hypothesis helps us understand why enzymes are highly specific. **(3 marks)**

Biology extended writing 1

When answering extended writing questions you should try to:

- ✓ Apply your scientific knowledge.
- ✓ Present your answer in a logical and organised way.
- ✓ Write a full answer and make sure that your spelling, punctuation and grammar are as good as you can make them.

Worked example

All living things are made from cells. However, there are differences between the cells of different organisms.

Compare the features of a typical bacterium with those of a typical animal cell. **(6 marks)**

Remember that a 'compare' question should include similarities *and* differences. In this case look at the features that are similar in animal cells and bacteria as well as the differences.

Sample answer 1

Bacteria are very small cells. There's not much in a bacteria cell – it doesn't have a nucleus really. It's just a blob of cytoplasm with a cell membrane. Some bacteria have got a tail on them.

This is a limited answer. It gives one or two points about bacteria, but doesn't compare them with animal cells. It could be improved by giving more detail of what is in both cells, and by using better scientific language (for instance, it would be better to say 'flagellum' rather than 'tail' in this context).

Sample answer 2

Animal cells and bacteria have some features in common. Both types of cell are made up of cytoplasm, surrounded by a cell membrane. However, most other features are different. For example, the animal cell has a nucleus, but the bacterium has the DNA free in the cytoplasm. This can either be in a big loop of chromosomal DNA, or a smaller ring of plasmid DNA. Animal cells have no cell wall, but bacteria may have a cell wall which is made of a slimy substance. Animal cells contain organelles such as mitochondria but bacteria do not have organelles. Bacteria also often have a flagellum which helps them move.

This is an excellent answer. It covers all the major points of difference between the two types of cell, as well as mentioning those features that are common.

Now try this

1. Describe the structure and function of the different parts of a typical plant cell. **(6 marks)**

Biology extended writing 2

Worked example

Although scientists have known about patterns of inheritance for many years, it took a long time to discover that inheritance was due to the molecule DNA. Biologists and chemists then worked for many more years to determine what a DNA molecule looked like.

Explain how the model we use to describe the DNA molecule has developed as a result of the work of different scientists. **(6 marks)**

Sample answer 1

DNA is made up of lots of bits linked together. Some of the sections of DNA are called genes and they come together to make DNA. DNA is a complicated spiral molecule, with two strands forming a helix structure. Lots of different scientists helped discover the structure. Watson and Crick got a Nobel prize for working it all out. Having lots of scientists all working together made it easier to get the right answer.

This is a limited answer. It could be improved by giving more detail of what the 'pieces' in DNA are and how the helix holds together. Although the answer is good because it talks about the collaboration between scientists, it does miss out the work done by Wilkins and Franklin.

Sample answer 2

The structure of DNA is referred to as a double helix. This means that there are two strands of the molecule twisted around side by side. The strands are made up of molecules which contain bases. These bases are A, C, T and G. The strands of DNA hold together because of hydrogen bonds between the bases. These bonds only form in certain ways. A bonds with T and C forms bonds with G. Many scientists were working on the structure of DNA. One pair was Wilkins and Franklin, who were using X-rays. Another group was Watson and Crick. Watson and Crick used information from the other scientists to help them work out the structure and build a model. Watson, Crick and Wilkins got a Nobel Prize.

This is an excellent answer. Note that it abbreviates the names of the bases – these could be written out in full to improve the answer even more. It credits the role of all the scientists involved in the discovery of DNA.

Now try this

1. Zymase is an enzyme found in yeast. It helps to break down glucose into ethanol and carbon dioxide. Describe how different factors can lead to zymase becoming less efficient at breaking down glucose. **(6 marks)**

Aerobic respiration

Respiration

All living organisms use respiration to release energy from organic molecules. The energy is used in the organism, for example, for growth and movement.

Aerobic respiration uses oxygen from the air to release energy from glucose. The products of aerobic respiration are carbon dioxide and water.

The reactions of aerobic respiration can be shown using a word equation:

glucose + oxygen → carbon dioxide + water (+ energy)

EXAM ALERT!

Make sure you know the difference between respiration (releasing energy in cells) and breathing (getting air into and out of the body). A question on this subject in a recent exam was only correctly answered by about two-fifths of students.

Students have struggled with this topic in recent exams - **be prepared!** ResultsPlus

Diffusion

Many substances enter and leave the body by diffusion. These substances include gases such as oxygen and carbon dioxide, and small digested food molecules such as glucose.

Before diffusion

The number of green particles decreases as you go down its concentration gradient.

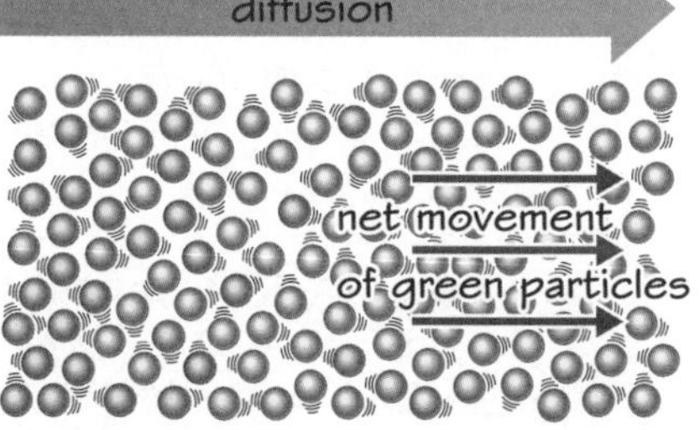

Diffusion is the net movement of particles from an area of higher concentration to an area of lower concentration. Particles are always moving and net movement is the sum of the movement of all particles.

Worked example

Complete the labels to show the role of the human circulatory system in supporting respiration.

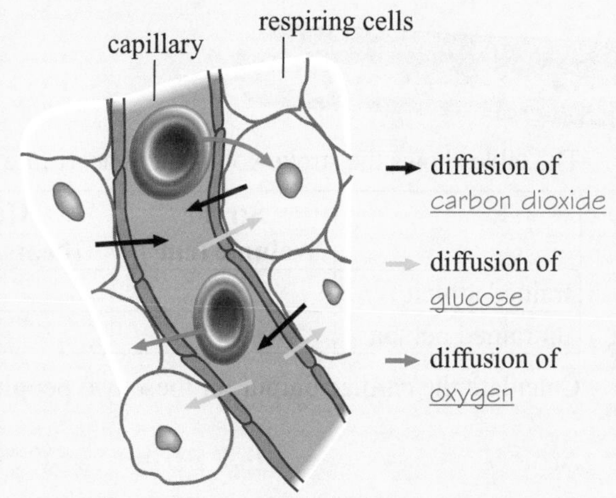

Now try this

target G-E

1. Copy and complete this word equation for aerobic respiration.

   glucose + _______ → carbon dioxide + _________ **(2 marks)**

target E-C

2. Explain why respiration is important in living organisms. **(2 marks)**
3. Explain why oxygen diffuses from the blood into respiring tissues. **(2 marks)**

Exercise

When you exercise, your heart rate and breathing rate increase. The harder you exercise, the more these rates increase.

Heart rate can be measured by taking your pulse at the wrist. It is usually measured as number of beats per minute. Breathing rate is measured by counting the number of breaths in one minute.

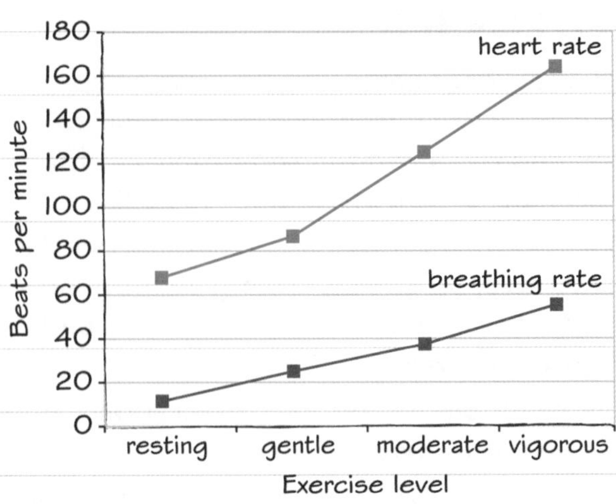

Heart rate and breathing rate can vary just by thinking about them. So take several measurements and average the results.

Why heart rate and breathing rate change

During exercise, muscle cells are respiring faster. This means that they need more oxygen and glucose and release more carbon dioxide:

A faster heart rate means that blood is pumped faster around the body. The blood takes oxygen and glucose to cells faster and removes carbon dioxide faster.

A faster breathing rate means that oxygen can be taken into the body at a faster rate and carbon dioxide can be released faster.

Worked example

The table shows the stroke volume and heart rate for two people at rest.

	Stroke volume (cm^3)	Heart rate (beats per minute)
trained athlete	90	55
untrained person	60	70

Calculate the cardiac output for these two people.

Athlete: $90 \times 55 = 4950\,cm^3$ per minute

Untrained person: $60 \times 70 = 4200\,cm^3$ per minute

cardiac output = stroke volume × heart rate

EXAM ALERT!

Show all your working for a calculation.

Students have struggled with exam questions similar to this - **be prepared!**

Now try this

1. (a) Describe one way of measuring breathing rate. **(1 mark)**
   (b) Describe one way of measuring heart rate. **(1 mark)**
2. Describe how heart rate varies with level of exercise. **(2 marks)**
3. Explain why breathing rate increases as level of exercise increases. **(2 marks)**

Anaerobic respiration

Anaerobic respiration is the release of energy from glucose without using oxygen. This produces lactic acid.

Anaerobic respiration can be shown using a word equation:

glucose → lactic acid (+ energy)

Aerobic respiration continues even when the cell uses anaerobic respiration. It's just that anaerobic respiration releases the extra energy the cell needs but can't get from aerobic respiration.

EXAM ALERT!

A recent exam question on this subject was only correctly answered by about two-fifths of students. Remember: anaerobic respiration in muscle cells produces *only one substance* – lactic acid.

Students have struggled with this topic in recent exams - **be prepared!** ResultsPlus

Advantage

✓ Anaerobic respiration is useful for muscle cells because it can release energy to allow muscles to contract when the heart and lungs cannot deliver oxygen and glucose fast enough for aerobic respiration.

Disadvantages

✗ Anaerobic respiration releases much less energy from each molecule of glucose than aerobic respiration.

✗ Lactic acid is not removed from the body. It builds up in muscle and blood, and must be broken down after exercise.

EPOC

Anyone who exercises hard will find that their heart and breathing rate take a while to return to their normal resting rate when exercise has ended. This is known as excess post-exercise oxygen consumption (EPOC).

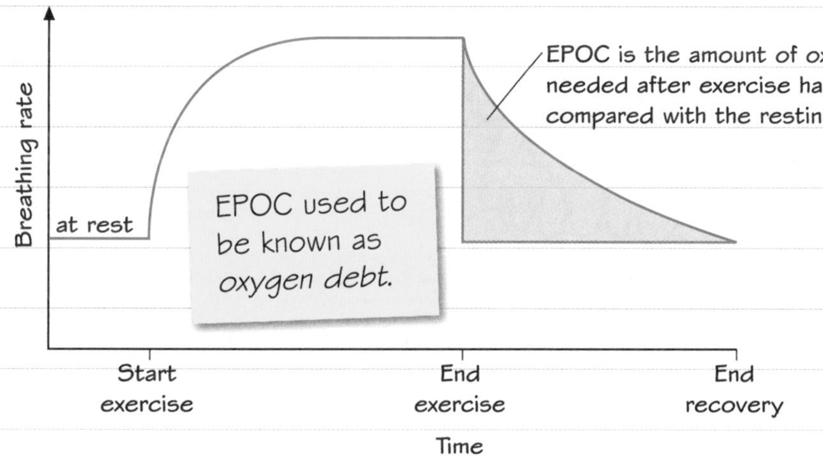
Breathing rate
at rest
EPOC is the amount of oxygen needed after exercise has ended compared with the resting rate.
EPOC used to be known as oxygen debt.
Start exercise
End exercise
End recovery
Time

Worked example

A student measured his resting pulse rate and breathing rate. Then he ran a 100 m sprint. After the race it took 5 minutes for his pulse and breathing rate to return to their resting rates. Explain why they didn't return to the resting rate as soon as the race finished.

Heart rate and breathing rate remain high after exercise to bring extra oxygen into the body. Some of this is needed to break down lactic acid produced from anaerobic respiration during the race.

Now try this

target G-E
target F-C
target E-C

1. Name the product of anaerobic respiration. **(1 mark)**
2. Define the term EPOC. **(2 marks)**
3. The EPOC of someone who has run fast for 10 minutes is greater than if they ran for 3 minutes. Explain why. **(3 marks)**

Photosynthesis

Photosynthesis is the process that plants use to make glucose. During this chemical reaction, light energy is used to combine carbon dioxide and water.

The process of photosynthesis can be shown by this word equation:

carbon dioxide + water $\xrightarrow{\text{energy from light}}$ glucose + oxygen

The glucose made during photosynthesis is used by the plant for respiration and other processes. Photosynthesis takes place in the light. Respiration happens all the time.

Adaptations for photosynthesis

Photosynthesis takes place in cells that are mostly found in leaves. Many leaves have a large surface area to capture as much light as possible for photosynthesis.

Worked example

The diagram shows a section through a leaf. Explain how the labelled structures are adaptations that help the plant to photosynthesise.

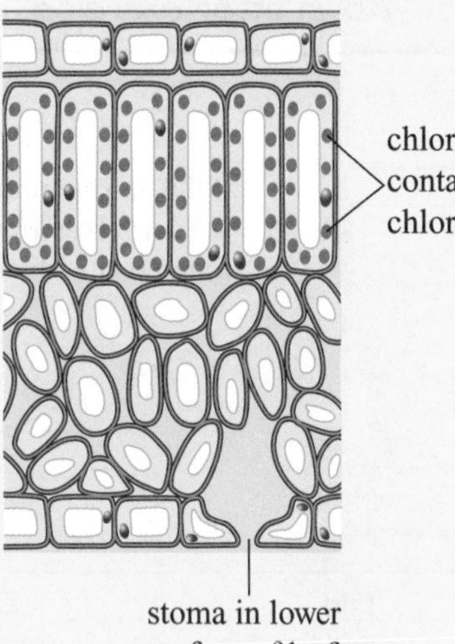

Chlorophyll in chloroplasts captures light energy needed for photosynthesis. The stomata in the leaf surface allow carbon dioxide needed for photosynthesis to diffuse into the leaf. They also allow oxygen and water vapour produced by photosynthesis to diffuse out of the leaf.

Remember: one **stoma**, two or more **stomata**.

You should mention diffusion when you are describing what stomata are for.

Now try this

1. Copy and complete this word equation for photosynthesis: **(2 marks)**
   carbon dioxide + ________ → glucose + ________
2. (a) Name the gas used in photosynthesis. **(1 mark)**
   (b) Explain how this gas gets into the leaf. **(3 marks)**
3. Explain why photosynthesis usually only takes place in some leaf cells. **(2 marks)**

Limiting factors

We can measure the effect of different factors on the rate of photosynthesis with this apparatus. The apparatus measures how much oxygen collects in an hour. The faster the oxygen is produced, the faster the rate of photosynthesis.

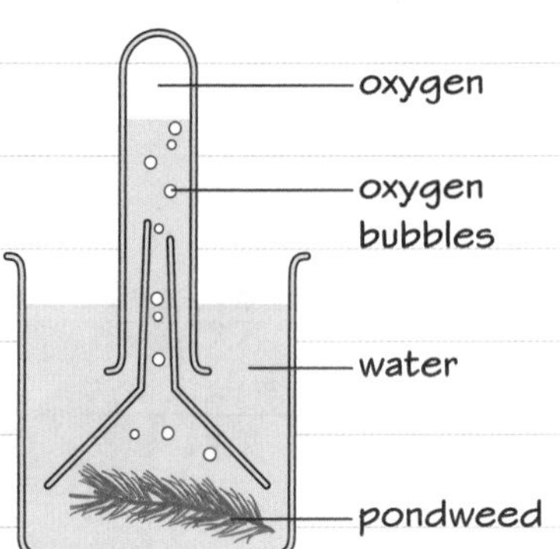

This apparatus can investigate the effect of:

- temperature using warm and cold water baths
- light intensity using bright and dim lights
- carbon dioxide concentration by adding different amounts of sodium hydrogen carbonate to the water.

Low temperature, dim light and low carbon dioxide concentration all *limit* the rate of photosynthesis. They are all limiting factors.

Worked example

The graph shows how the rate of photosynthesis changes with light intensity. Explain the shape of the graph at points A and B.

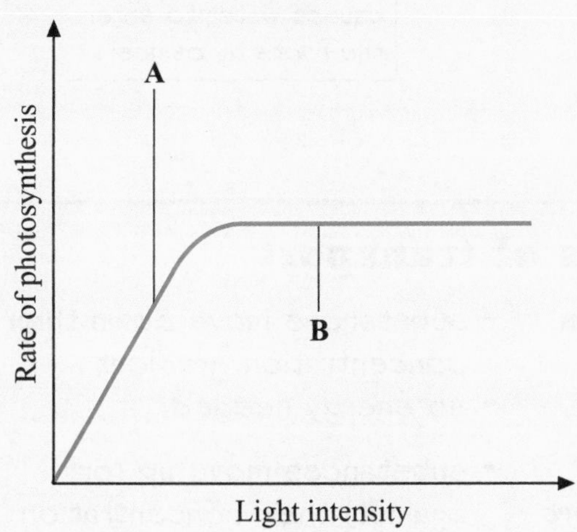

At A, light intensity is limiting photosynthesis, because increasing the light intensity increases the rate of photosynthesis. At B, light intensity is no longer the limiting factor because increasing the light intensity does not change the rate of photosynthesis.

EXAM ALERT!

A question on a recent exam asked about limiting factors and around two out of three students did not get any marks at all. When answering questions on limiting factors remember that light intensity is not the only factor that limits the rate of photosynthesis. Temperature and carbon dioxide concentration are important too.

Students have struggled with exam questions similar to this - **be prepared!**

Increasing only carbon dioxide concentration or temperature, while keeping other factors constant, will produce a similar graph to this.

Now try this

1. State three factors that can affect the rate of photosynthesis. **(3 marks)**
2. Define the term *limiting factor*. **(2 marks)**

3. Explain why measuring the oxygen given off by a plant is a way of measuring the rate of photosynthesis. **(2 marks)**

Water transport

Water and substances dissolved in the water are transported around plants in veins. Veins contain tissues called xylem and phloem.

glucose, produced by photosynthesis in leaves, is converted to sucrose, which is transported in phloem to the rest of the plant

water and dissolved minerals from the roots travel in xylem to the rest of the plant

water and dissolved minerals enter plants through their roots from the soil water

Transpiration

Transpiration is the evaporation of water from inside leaves out into the air. It causes water to move up the plant from the roots.

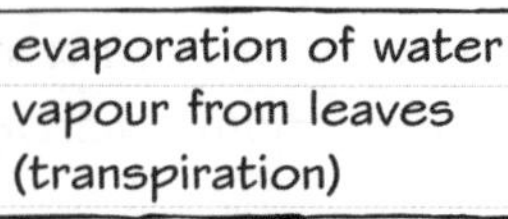

↓

draws water out of the leaf cells and xylem

↓

draws water up the xylem from the roots

↓

causes water to enter the roots by osmosis

Worked example

Explain the meaning of the phrase *active transport*. Use minerals entering roots as your example.

Mineral salts cannot enter the root cells from soil water by diffusion because there is a higher concentration of mineral salts in the cells than in the soil. So the root cells have to use energy to transport mineral salts into the cells against their concentration gradient.

Types of transport

Diffusion
- substances move down their concentration gradient
- no energy needed

Active transport
- substances move up (or against) their concentration gradient
- needs energy so substances can move

Osmosis = diffusion of water molecules (opposite page)

Now try this

1. **(a)** Name one substance that moves up a plant in xylem. **(1 mark)**
   (b) Identify where this substance came from, before it got into the plant. **(1 mark)**
2. Name the two tissues that make up the veins in plants. **(2 marks)**

target E-C

3. **(a)** Define the term transpiration. **(1 mark)**
   (b) Describe the role of transpiration in the movement of water through a plant. **(2 marks)**

Osmosis

Osmosis is the net movement of water molecules from a region of their higher concentration to a region of their lower concentration through a partially permeable membrane.

A partially permeable membrane is a membrane that lets some molecules through but not others. Cell membranes are partially permeable membranes because small molecules pass through but not bigger molecules.

Osmosis is a special case of diffusion – it is the diffusion of water.

Osmosis can be investigated using potato strips or red onion cells in solutions of different concentrations.

At the start

a concentrated sugar solution contains many sugar molecules and some water molecules

a dilute sugar solution contains many water molecules and some sugar molecules

water molecule

sugar molecule

partially permeable membrane

all molecules are moving

After a few minutes

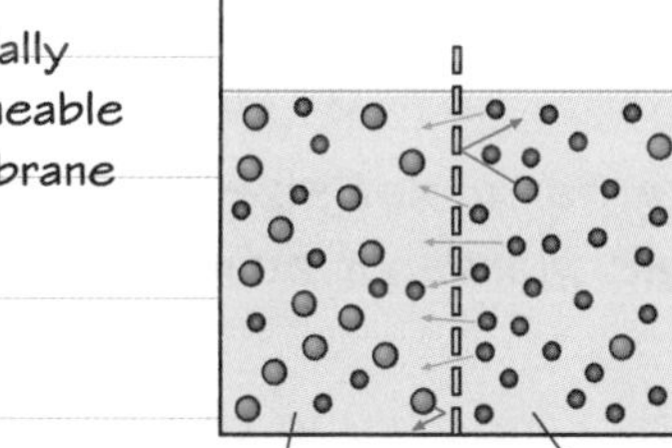

a few water molecules means only a few cross through the membrane

lots of water molecules means lots cross through the membrane

After a while

water molecules are small enough to pass through the membrane, while suga molecules are too large

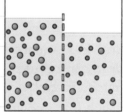

Worked example

The diagram shows two root hairs on the outside of a root. Describe how these cells are adapted to take up water by osmosis.

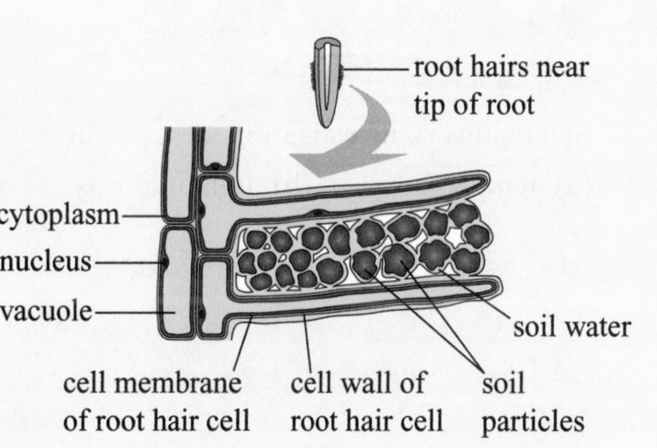

Root hair cells have long extensions that stretch out into the soil. This gives them a large surface area where osmosis can take place, which means that more water molecules can cross the cell membrane into the cell at the same time.

Now try this

target G-E

1. Complete the sentence.
   Osmosis is the diffusion of _______ molecules across a partially ______ membrane. **(2 marks)**

target F-C

2. Write a definition for *osmosis*. **(3 marks)**

3. Look at the diagram at the top of the page. Explain why the level of solution rises on one side of the membrane and falls on the other after a while. **(3 marks)**

Organisms and the environment

When you carry out fieldwork to investigate the relationship between organisms and their environment, you need suitable equipment and sampling techniques.

Collecting animals

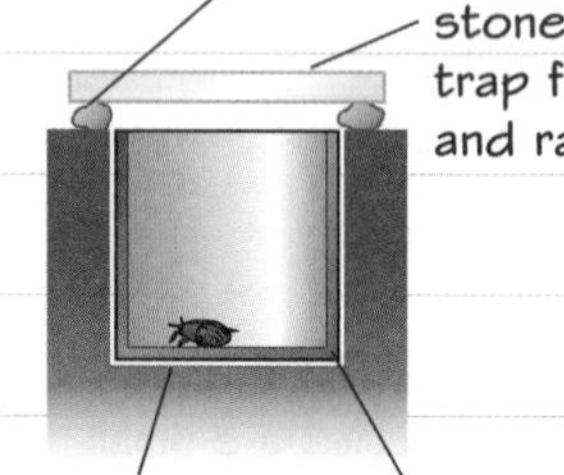
small stones support lid off the ground so animals can fall into trap
stone lid shelters trap from sun and rain
hole in ground
container

pitfall trap
for collecting small ground-living animals

sweep through grass and bushes or through water in pond or stream

sweep net or pond net
for collecting larger animals

inlet tube

mouth piece

a suck on the mouthpiece draws the animal in through the inlet tube

net to stop the animals getting into your mouth

pooter
for collecting animals smaller than the inlet tube

Quadrats

A quadrat is a square frame of a particular size (e.g. 50 cm^2). A quadrat can be used to sample plants or animals that don't move much. To get good results:

- each quadrat should be placed randomly in the sample area
- count the number of organisms, or estimate the area covered by the organism, in each quadrat
- repeat the measurement in several quadrats
- calculate an average measurement for one quadrat.

Quadrats can also be used to sample organisms along a straight line – to see how the distribution of organisms changes along the line.

Environmental factors

Worked example

In a fieldwork investigation, describe how you would measure these environmental factors:

(a) temperature **(b)** light intensity **(c)** pH of soil.

(a) Temperature probe connected to a datalogger, or a thermometer.

(b) Light probe connected to a datalogger, or a light meter.

(c) Mix a sample of soil with distilled water, then measure the pH of the solution with Universal indicator or a pH probe.

Now try this

target
G-D

1. Identify the best equipment to collect a sample of small beetles. **(1 mark)**
2. Explain why a pitfall trap should be covered. **(1 mark)**

target E-C

3. Explain why it is good practice to sample using several quadrats in an area, and then average the results from each quadrat. **(2 marks)**

Biology extended writing 3

Worked example

The boys in a class measured their heart rate. They then exercised for a 5-minute period and measured their heart rate again.

The mean (average) heart rate of the boys at rest was 65 beats per minute. After exercise, the mean (average) heart rate was 97.

Explain why the heart rate of the boys changed as they took exercise. **(6 marks)**

Sample answer 1

When they did exercise, the boys were using energy. They need more energy if they are exercising for a long time, so their hearts beat faster. The boys' heart rate went up from 32 beats per minute. That's half as much again from where it started.

This is a basic answer. It is always good to use some of the data from a question like this. However, in this question the answer doesn't use the data correctly (the heart rate went up *by* 32 beats per minute, not *from* 32 beats per minute) and very little has been added to the answer by using the data like this. To improve, the answer could talk about the process that releases the energy.

Sample answer 2

When the boys exercise, their muscles will work much harder. To do this work, the cells in the muscles need lots of energy. They do this through a process called respiration. Aerobic respiration in the muscle cells needs two things – glucose and oxygen. Both of these are supplied to the muscles by the blood. So, to exercise harder, the boys' muscles need blood more quickly. The boys measured the increase in their heart rate – this means that the heart is pumping more often. So, the boys' heart rate goes up with exercise, to get more blood to the muscle cells. This increased blood flow also takes away the waste materials from the muscle cells.

This is an excellent answer. Most importantly, it answers the question asked, by discussing how the muscles have a bigger demand for the glucose and oxygen carried in the blood. It gives the additional information that this is aerobic respiration. Also, it mentions the idea that increased blood flow is important in removing waste materials from the muscles to prevent fatigue.

Now try this

1. Plants have leaves that are adapted to carry out the process of photosynthesis. Describe how a leaf is adapted for efficient photosynthesis. **(6 marks)**

You could start your answer by saying what happens in photosynthesis. Then you can continue by writing about how the different structures in the leaf help with photosynthesis.

Fossils and evolution

Fossils are the preserved traces or remains of organisms that lived thousands or millions of years ago. The fossil record in rocks gives us evidence of what the living organisms were like and how they changed over time. This is called evolution.

Gaps in the fossil record

The fossil record is not complete. There are several reasons for this.

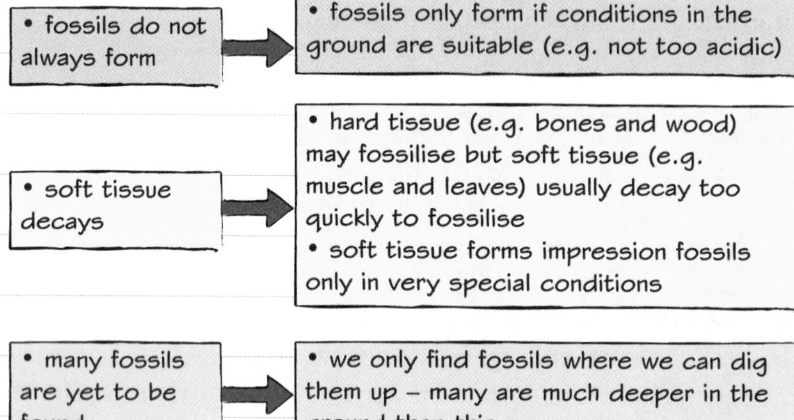

• fossils do not always form
• fossils only form if conditions in the ground are suitable (e.g. not too acidic)
• soft tissue decays
• hard tissue (e.g. bones and wood) may fossilise but soft tissue (e.g. muscle and leaves) usually decay too quickly to fossilise
• soft tissue forms impression fossils only in very special conditions
• many fossils are yet to be found
• we only find fossils where we can dig them up – many are much deeper in the ground than this

Worked example

The diagram shows the skeleton and outline of a fossil of a whale ancestor and of a modern whale. Describe the evidence shown by the fossil for the evolution of whales.

The fossil shows that whales evolved from animals that had teeth in their jaws and legs that were adapted for moving on land.

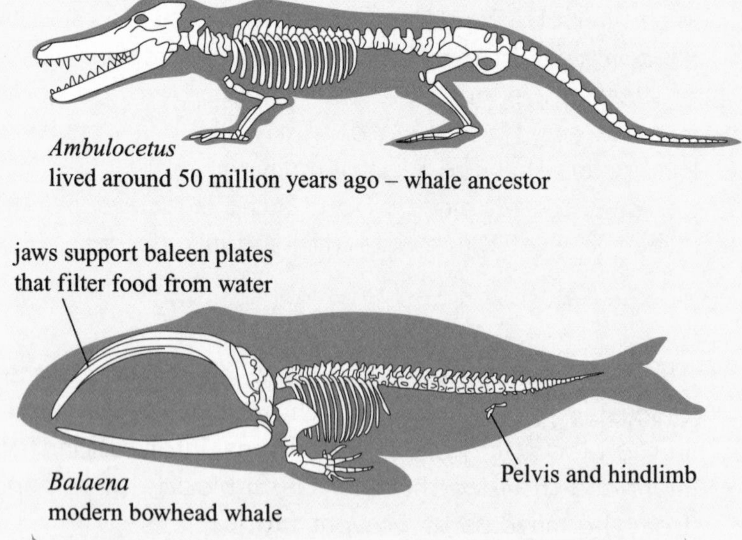

Ambulocetus
lived around 50 million years ago – whale ancestor

Balaena
modern bowhead whale

Now try this

1. Explain what we mean by the *fossil record*. **(2 marks)**
2. Give two reasons why the fossil record is not complete. **(2 marks)**

3. Explain how fossils can give us evidence for evolution. **(2 marks)**

Growth

When organisms grow they get bigger. Growth can be measured in different ways.

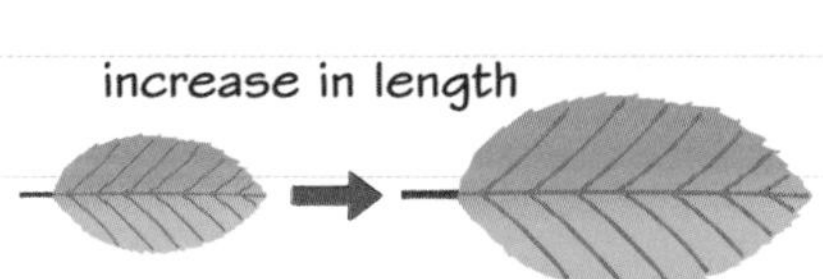

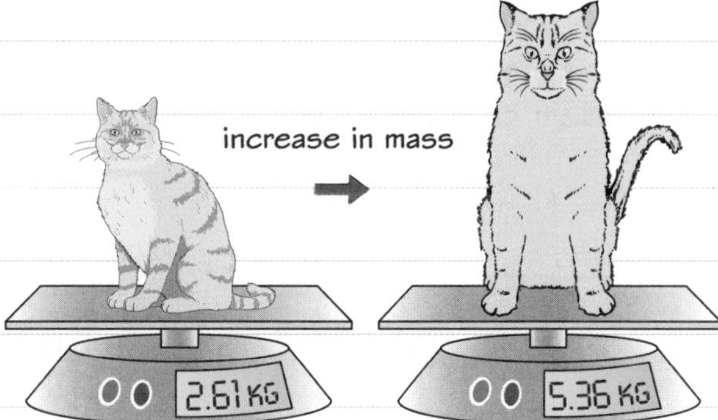

Growth is a *permanent* increase in size. For example, a balloon that is blown up a little more has not 'grown' in size.

Percentile charts

Percentile charts can help to show if a child is growing faster or slower than is normal for their age.

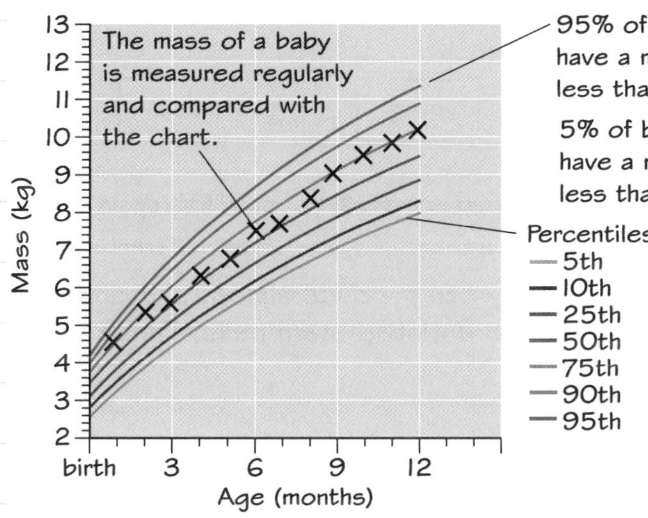

Babies with a mass above the 95th line or below the 5th line may not be growing properly.

A baby whose mass decreases by two or more percentiles over their first year may not be growing normally.

The chart is for baby girls. The chart for baby boys is similar, but they grow at a slightly different rate to girls.

Worked example

Look at the percentile chart. The crosses mark the mass of a baby girl measured each month.

(a) State the percentile that she belonged to in her first month.

(a) 75th percentile.

(b) Do you think there was concern about this baby's mass increase in her first year? Explain your answer.

(b) No, because her mass varied only between the 75th and 50th percentiles, and this amount of variation is normal.

Now try this

1. Write a definition of *growth* in your own words. **(1 mark)**

2. (a) Describe one way in which you could measure the growth of a plant. **(1 mark)**

(b) Explain how you would know that growth was taking place. **(2 marks)**

3. Describe what a *percentile chart* shows and what it can be used for. **(2 marks)**

Growth of plants and animals

Growth and development in plants

A meristem is the part of a plant shoot or root just behind the tip. Plant growth includes cell division at the meristem, and cell elongation (the cells get longer) further away from the meristem. Meristem cells are all the same. They can develop into any kind of cell in a plant.

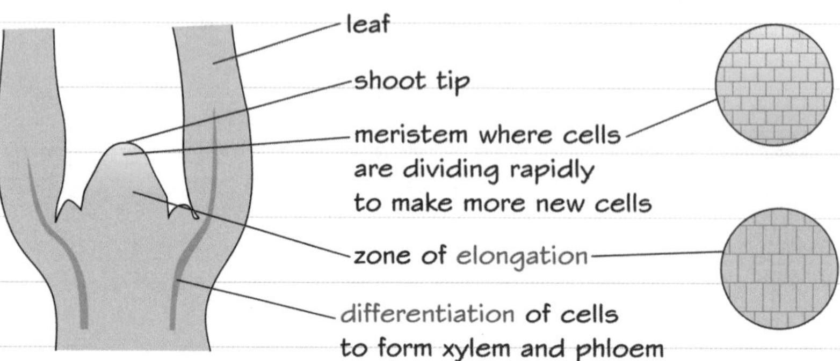

Growth and development in animals

Animals grow in a different way from plants. As the animal gets older, most of the cells in their body differentiate into specialised cells, such as muscle, bone or nerve cells.

embryo → birth → young → adult

cell division: very rapid for growth → slow for repair

cell differentiation: not differentiated → most differentiated

All the cells in an embryo are stem cells. This means they can produce almost any kind of cell. Only a few cells in a child or adult's body are undifferentiated stem cells. These stem cells help to repair damaged tissue.

Worked example

Compare the growth and differentiation of cells in plants and animals.

Plants produce new cells at their shoot and root tips throughout and continue growing all their lives. Differentiation of plant cells happens behind the shoot or root tips.
Growth by cell division in animals is rapid in the embryo but gets slower as the animal gets older. Cells differentiate as the animal gets older until only a few stem cells are left.

Now try this

1. Plants grow by *cell division* and *cell elongation*. Explain the difference between these terms. **(2 marks)**
2. Explain what is meant by *cell differentiation* in animals. **(1 mark)**
3. Plant meristem cells are like animal stem cells. Explain what this means. **(1 mark)**

Blood

Blood is made of four main parts: plasma, red blood cells, white blood cells and platelets. Each part of blood has a particular function (job).

Blood plasma

Plasma is the liquid part of blood:

- It carries the blood cells through the blood vessels.
- It contains many dissolved substances, such as carbon dioxide and glucose.

plasma (55%)
white blood cells and platelets (<1%)
red blood cells (45%)

White blood cells

White blood cells are larger than red blood cells, and they have a nucleus. All types of white blood cells are part of the immune system that attacks pathogens in the body.

nucleus

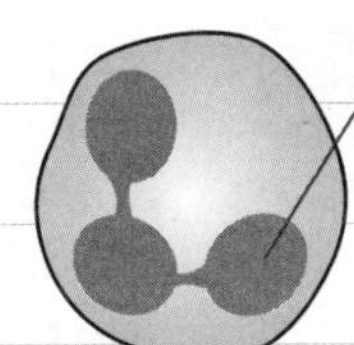

Some white blood cells surround and destroy pathogens.

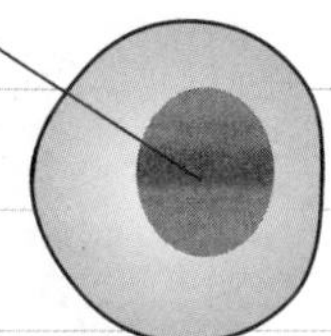

Some white blood cells produce antibodies that destroy pathogens.

Platelets

Platelets are fragments of larger cells. They have no nucleus. Their function is to cause blood to clot when a blood vessel has been damaged. The clot blocks the wound and prevents pathogens getting into the blood.

Worked example

Complete the labels on the diagram of a red blood cell to show how the structure of the cell is related to its function.

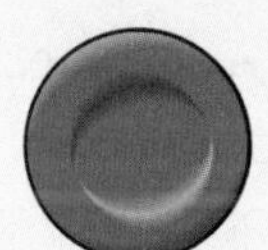

The red colour is caused by a chemical called haemoglobin.
The function of this chemical is to carry oxygen.

The cell has a biconcave shape (dimple on each side). So the cell has a large surface area for oxygen to diffuse across.

The cell has no nucleus. This means the cell has room for more haemoglobin.

Now try this

1. Respiring cells need oxygen and glucose. Identify the parts of the blood that carry each of these substances. **(2 marks)**

target E-C

2. Describe two ways in which white blood cells protect us from pathogens. **(2 marks)**

The heart

Cells are grouped into tissues and tissues are grouped into organs. The heart is an organ that contains tissues such as heart muscle and tendons. Heart muscle is formed from heart muscle cells.

Structure and function of the heart

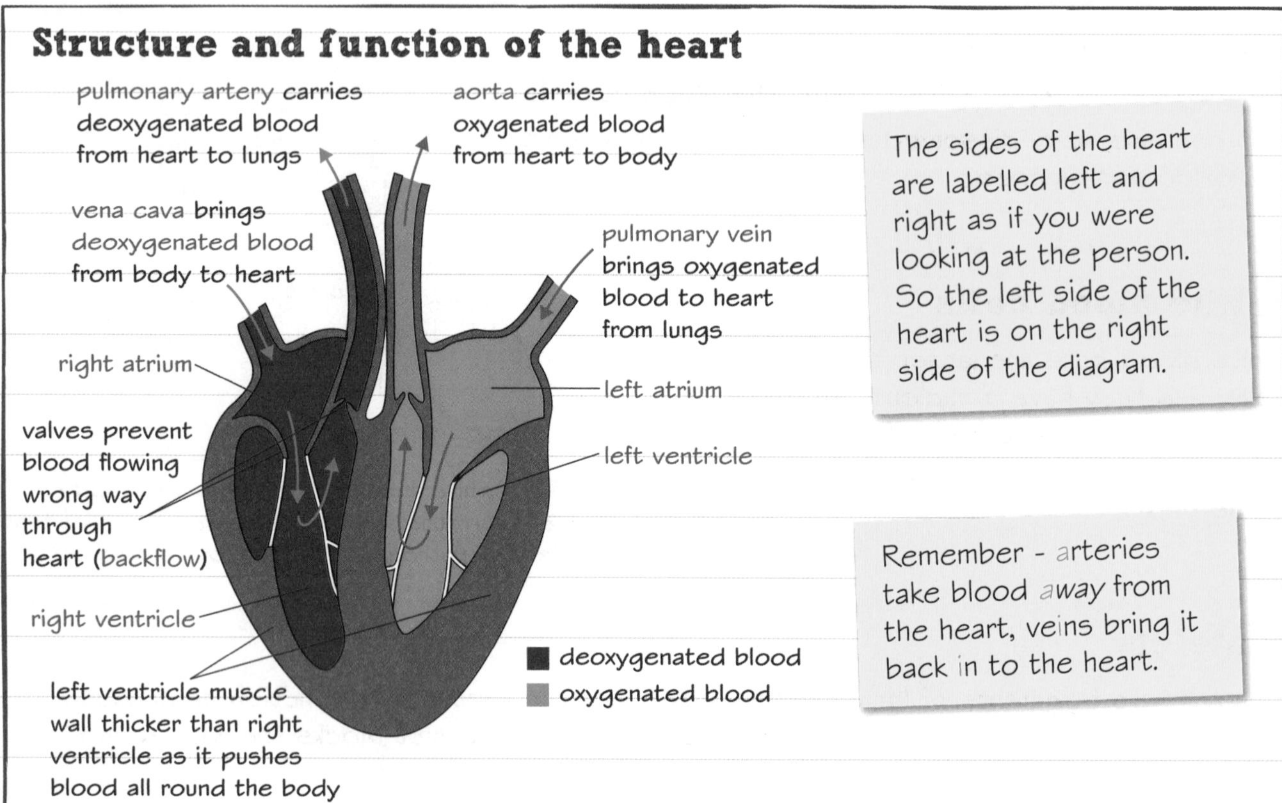
pulmonary artery carries deoxygenated blood from heart to lungs
aorta carries oxygenated blood from heart to body
vena cava brings deoxygenated blood from body to heart
pulmonary vein brings oxygenated blood to heart from lungs
right atrium
left atrium
valves prevent blood flowing wrong way through heart (backflow)
left ventricle
right ventricle
left ventricle muscle wall thicker than right ventricle as it pushes blood all round the body
deoxygenated blood
oxygenated blood
The sides of the heart are labelled left and right as if you were looking at the person. So the left side of the heart is on the right side of the diagram.
Remember - arteries take blood away from the heart, veins bring it back in to the heart.

Worked example

Complete the flow chart to identify the direction of blood flow through the blood vessels supplying the heart and the main parts of the heart, and whether the blood is oxygenated or deoxygenated.

deoxygenated blood

blood enters the heart through the vena cava	→	blood is pumped through the right atrium and then through the right ventricle	→	blood leaves the heart through the pulmonary artery

oxygenated blood

blood enters the heart through the pulmonary vein	→	blood is pumped through the left atrium and then through the left ventricle	→	blood leaves the heart through the aorta

Oxygenated blood contains a higher concentration of oxygen than deoxygenated blood.

Now try this

target G-D

1. Name one tissue found in the heart. **(1 mark)**
2. (a) Explain why there are valves in the heart. **(2 marks)**

target E-C

(b) Explain why the left ventricle wall contains more muscle than the right ventricle wall. **(2 marks)**

The circulatory system

An organ system is a group of organs that work together to carry out a particular function in the body. The circulatory system is an organ system that consists of the heart, the blood vessels and the blood. Its function is to transport materials around the body.

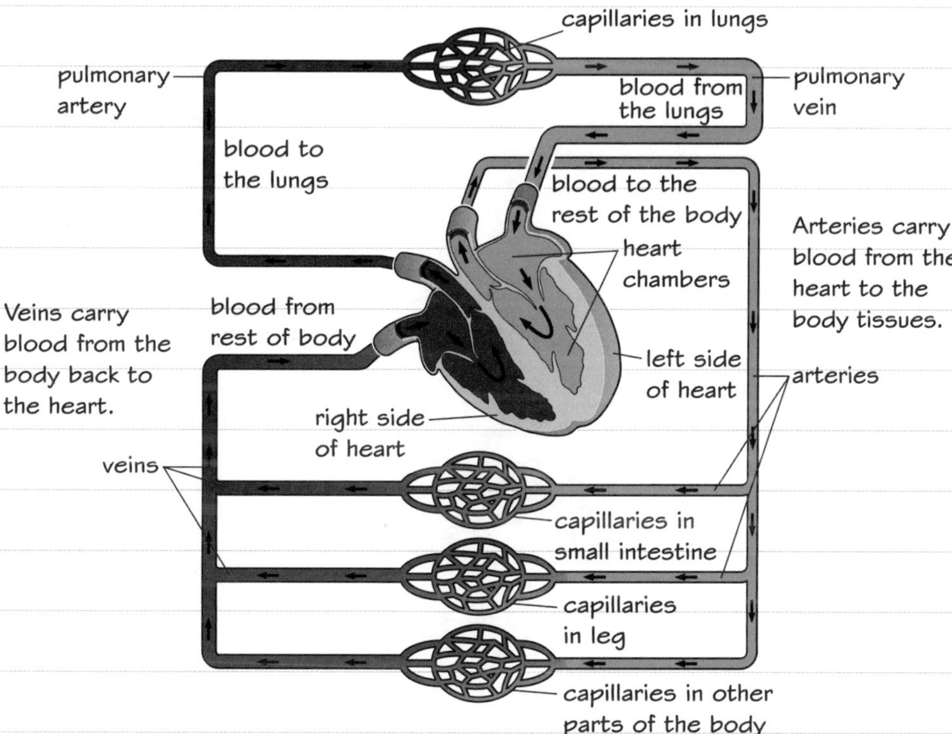

Worked example

The blood in capillaries exchanges materials with the tissues it flows through.

(a) Explain what happens to oxygen as blood in capillaries flows through a tissue.

(a) Oxygen diffuses from the blood into the cells for use in respiration.

(b) Explain what happens to carbon dioxide as blood flows through a tissue in capillaries.

(b) Carbon dioxide diffuses out of cells where it is formed in respiration. It diffuses into the blood for transport to the lungs where it is excreted.

During respiration, oxygen reacts with glucose to release energy and produce carbon dioxide and water (see page 17).

Now try this

1. Name one organ in the circulatory system. **(1 mark)**

2. The aorta is the first blood vessel that blood enters after leaving the heart. Is the aorta an artery or vein? Explain your answer. **(2 marks)**

3. Describe the role of the circulatory system in the body. **(2 marks)**

The digestive system

There are many organs in the digestive system. These organs work together to digest food and allow food molecules to be absorbed into the body.

mouth
• food enters the body
• chewing breaks up food and mixes it with enzymes to start digestion

oesophagus
• carries food from mouth to stomach

food moving down oesophagus

liver
• produces bile, which helps in digestion of fats in small intestine
• converts food molecules absorbed from small intestine into other molecules

stomach
• acid and enzymes added
• stomach contents mixed by churning of muscular wall

pancreas
• produces enzymes that are released into the small intestine

small intestine
• digestion of food by enzymes completed
• food molecules are absorbed into the blood
• water absorbed from digested food

large intestine
• some water absorbed
• undigested food forms faeces that pass out of body through anus

anus

Worked example

Explain how food is moved through the alimentary canal.

Food moves through the alimentary canal by peristalsis. Peristalsis is the contraction of some muscles in the wall of the alimentary canal, and relaxation of others, which pushes the food along from the oesophagus to the anus.

The alimentary canal is the tube between the mouth and the anus that the food passes through.

Now try this

1. Name two organs in the digestive system. **(2 marks)**
2. Name the part of the digestive system where digested food is absorbed. **(1 mark)**

3. Describe the role of the liver in the digestive system. **(2 marks)**

Breaking down food

Our food contains carbohydrates, proteins and fats. These molecules are too large to be absorbed into the body. Digestive enzymes in the alimentary canal digest large food molecules into small molecules that can be absorbed.

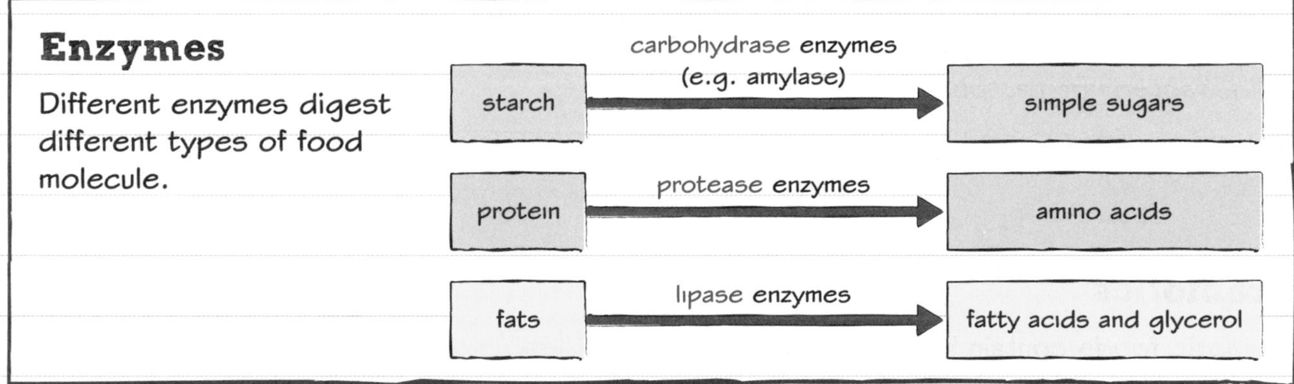

Enzymes

Different enzymes digest different types of food molecule.

Model of the alimentary canal

Visking tubing can be used in investigations of diffusion. It makes a good model for the alimentary canal because small molecules like glucose can diffuse through it but large molecules like starch cannot.

boiling tube
beaker
Visking tubing
mixture of starch and amylase
water at 30°C
At start: water
At end: glucose has diffused out of bag into the water

Worked example

Use the graph to help you describe the effect of enzyme concentration on the rate of a reaction.

The reaction goes faster with a greater enzyme concentration.

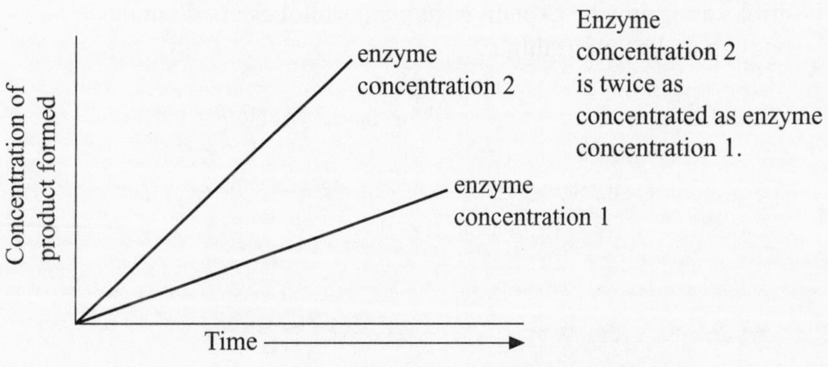

Enzyme concentration 2 is twice as concentrated as enzyme concentration 1.

Now try this

1. Name the group of enzymes that digest proteins. **(1 mark)**
2. Name the molecules produced when a lipase enzyme digests a fat molecule. **(2 marks)**
3. Name one example of a carbohydrase. **(1 mark)**

4. Explain why we need digestive enzymes. **(2 marks)**

Probiotics and prebiotics

Functional foods are foods that claim to make you healthier when you eat them.

Probiotics

Probiotic foods contain 'friendly' bacteria that are usually either *Bifidobacteria* or *Lactobacillus*.

manufacturer claim:
makes you healthier by improving your digestive system and immune system

scientific studies show:
little or no evidence to support these claims

Prebiotics

Prebiotic foods contain high levels of oligosaccharides.

health claim:
prebiotic oligosaccharides encourage beneficial bacteria to grow in your alimentary canal, which can protect you from problems such as diarrhoea

scientific studies show:
there is increasing evidence that prebiotics improve health by reducing the risk of diarrhoea and other problems

Worked example

Plant stanol esters are used as functional foods in yogurt, drinks and spreads. Explain what plant stanol esters do in the body to make you healthier.

Plant stanol esters reduce the amount of cholesterol absorbed from digested food. Reducing the amount of blood cholesterol may reduce your chance of having heart disease.

There is evidence that plant stanol esters reduce the amount of cholesterol in the blood. Scientists are still testing whether they also reduce the risk of heart disease.

Now try this

1. State one group of functional foods. **(1 mark)**
2. Explain how prebiotic foods are supposed to make you healthier. **(1 mark)**

3. Use the information on this page to give an example of a functional food and any scientific evidence to support the claim that it makes you healthier. Explain your answer. **(2 marks)**

Biology extended writing 4

Worked example

Your friend, Will, has caught the flu and goes to see his doctor. His doctor tells him that his white blood cells will help him fight the flu virus. Will didn't realise that blood contained different components. He asks you about the components of blood.

Write a description of the other components of the blood, outlining the different functions they carry out. **(6 marks)**

Sample answer 1

Blood contains white blood cells, red blood cells and platelets. White blood cells are part of our defence system. They make antibodies and help us fight infection. Red blood cells are very different. They help carry oxygen around the body, because they contain haemoglobin. Red blood cells are specially shaped to help them get into even the smallest blood vessels. Platelets aren't proper cells – they are just bits of cells.

This is a basic answer. Note that the information about white blood cells would not score any marks - the question asks only about the **other** components of the blood. There is a good description of red blood cells. To improve, the answer could give some information about the role of the platelets. It also does not mention the largest component of the blood!

Sample answer 2

PLASMA – Most of the blood is plasma. Plasma is the liquid part of the blood and it carries most of the nutrients and other dissolved substances like hormones.

RED BLOOD CELLS – These are the next biggest component in blood. These cells have no nucleus! But they have an important job – they have haemoglobin, which helps them carry oxygen around the body.

PLATELETS – These are fragments of cells. Their job is to make sure that we form blood clots if we cut ourselves. This stops us bleeding to death! It also helps keep bacteria out.

This is a good answer. Remember that in an exam you don't have much time to write your answer to questions like this. It can help to structure your answer in a simple way like this, but don't forget to use whole sentences.

This answer mentions all three components of the blood and gives some detail about each one. But even though it is an excellent answer, there are things that it misses out. For example, it could give more detail about the structure of the red blood cells.

Now try this

1. Ahmed eats a bowl of rice. Describe what happens to the starch in the rice as it passes through Ahmed's digestive system. **(6 marks)**

Biology extended writing 5

Worked example

Humans grow from around 50 cm as babies to around 175 cm as adults.

Oak trees may grow up to 20 m tall from a very small acorn.

Explain the similarities and differences in the way in which plants and animals grow. **(6 marks)**

Sample answer 1

Both plants and animals grow when their cells divide. This happens when the cells split to form daughter cells. In plants, the growth happens at the ends of shoots or roots. This makes the roots grow further into the ground or the shoots grow up into the air. Animals tend to have more different types of cell. These cells all grow, but this growth is slower. Animal cells are more specialised.

This is a basic answer. Although it appears to give several key points, much of what it says repeats itself or repeats the question. The answer could be improved by using scientific words – for example, naming the sort of cell division, or the cells that cause growth in plants. There could also be more detail on the difference between plant and animal growth using stem cells and the fact that plant cells use elongation.

Sample answer 2

The most common form of growth is through cell division. For most cells, this happens by mitosis. Plants cells can also elongate. Most of this growth happens at the tips of the plants. Plants also have some special cells that can turn into many different types of cells – that's why plants will grow from cuttings because these cells can turn into roots, leaves or stems.

Humans also grow through cell division. Human body cells are made through mitosis, just like plant cells, but they do not elongate like plants cells. Animals also have stem cells. Stem cells in human embryos are not differentiated – they can turn into any adult cells. Adult stem cells can only turn into a limited number of cells.

This is a good answer. It describes the common features in the growth of plants and animals, as well as giving very good detail about the differences. There is excellent coverage of the importance of stem cells. What makes this answer especially good is the use of appropriate scientific terminology, such as 'mitosis', 'stem cells' and 'differentiate'.

Now try this

1. The circulatory system in the human body carries blood with nutrients and oxygen to our cells. Describe how the circulatory system is designed to transport blood around the body. **(6 marks)**

Structure of the atom

Atoms are the smallest part of elements that can take part in chemical reactions.

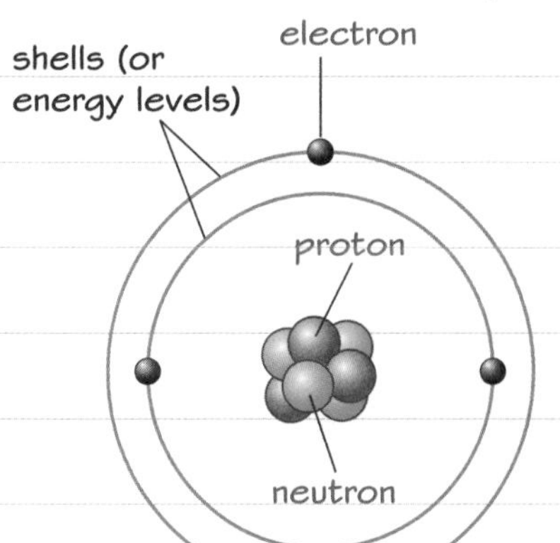

Atoms of a given element all have the same number of protons in their nuclei. It is the number of protons in the nucleus that determines which element the atom is part of.

This diagram is not to scale. The nucleus of an atom is tiny compared with the overall size of the atom. It is only about 1/20 000th of the size of the atom!

Protons, neutrons and electrons

Particle	Relative mass	Relative charge
proton	1	+1
neutron	1	0
electron	1/1850	−1

The masses and charges on subatomic particles are very small, so we only talk about the masses and charges *relative* to each other. The mass of an electron is so small that we don't bother to account for it in calculations.

Atoms have the same number of protons and electrons. The + charges on the protons balance the − charges on the electrons, so the atom is neutral overall.

Worked example

An atom of sodium has 11 protons in its nucleus and 12 neutrons.

(a) What is its atomic number?

(a) 11

(b) What is its mass number?

(b) 23

The **atomic number** of an element is the number of protons in the nucleus. The **mass number** is the total number of protons and neutrons in the nucleus.

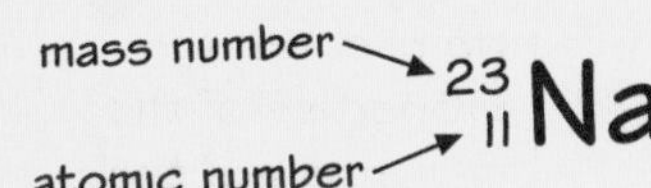

The masses of atoms are so small that we do not talk about their mass in kilograms. Instead we use **relative atomic mass**. Carbon is the element with which all others are compared.

Now try this

target G-E

1. **(a)** Give the name of the particles found in the nucleus of atoms. **(2 marks)**
   (b) Name the particles in an atom that have an electrical charge, and state the charges. **(2 marks)**

target G-D

2. An atom of fluorine has 9 protons and 10 neutrons. State its atomic number and mass number. **(2 marks)**

The modern periodic table

The elements in the modern periodic table are arranged in order of their atomic numbers.

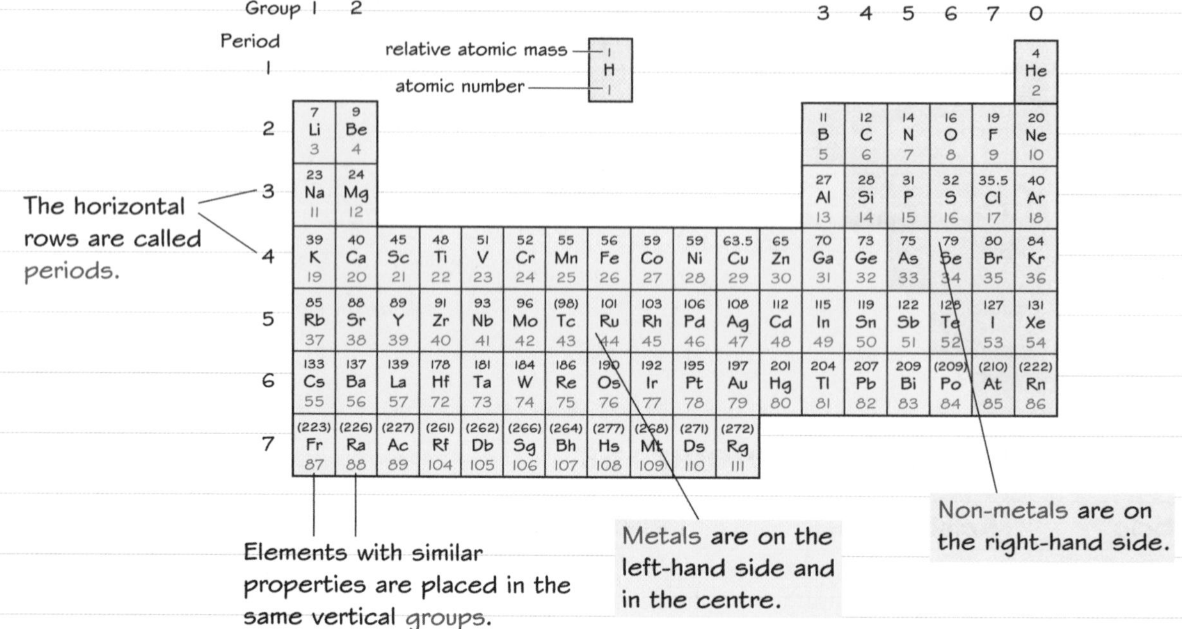

Period	Group 1	2											3	4	5	6	7	0
1								1 H 1										4 He 2
2	7 Li 3	9 Be 4											11 B 5	12 C 6	14 N 7	16 O 8	19 F 9	20 Ne 10
3	23 Na 11	24 Mg 12											27 Al 13	28 Si 14	31 P 15	32 S 16	35.5 Cl 17	40 Ar 18
4	39 K 19	40 Ca 20	45 Sc 21	48 Ti 22	51 V 23	52 Cr 24	55 Mn 25	56 Fe 26	59 Co 27	59 Ni 28	63.5 Cu 29	65 Zn 30	70 Ga 31	73 Ge 32	75 As 33	79 Se 34	80 Br 35	84 Kr 36
5	85 Rb 37	88 Sr 38	89 Y 39	91 Zr 40	93 Nb 41	96 Mo 42	(98) Tc 43	101 Ru 44	103 Rh 45	106 Pd 46	108 Ag 47	112 Cd 48	115 In 49	119 Sn 50	122 Sb 51	128 Te 52	127 I 53	131 Xe 54
6	133 Cs 55	137 Ba 56	139 La 57	178 Hf 72	181 Ta 73	184 W 74	186 Re 75	190 Os 76	192 Ir 77	195 Pt 78	197 Au 79	201 Hg 80	204 Tl 81	207 Pb 82	209 Bi 83	(209) Po 84	(210) At 85	(222) Rn 86
7	(223) Fr 87	(226) Ra 88	(227) Ac 89	(261) Rf 104	(262) Db 105	(266) Sg 106	(264) Bh 107	(277) Hs 108	(268) Mt 109	(271) Ds 110	(272) Rg 111							

relative atomic mass
atomic number
The horizontal rows are called periods.
Elements with similar properties are placed in the same vertical groups.
Metals are on the left-hand side and in the centre.
Non-metals are on the right-hand side.

Mendeleev

The periodic table as we know it was first made by Mendeleev, who arranged all the elements known at the time into a table.

Mendeleev put the elements in order of the relative atomic mass.

→ He checked the properties of the elements and their compounds.

→ He swapped the places of some elements so that elements with similar properties lined up.

→ He left gaps where he thought there were other elements, and predicted their properties.

→ When these elements were discovered, Mendeleev's predictions fitted the properties very well!

Now try this

target
G-E

1. Write the symbol of an element that is:
   (a) in the same group as lithium (Li) **(1 mark)**
   (b) in the same period as lithium. **(1 mark)**
2. Explain how you can tell from the periodic table that lithium is a metal. **(2 marks)**
3. The atomic number of potassium is 19.
   (a) State the symbol for potassium. **(1 mark)**
   (b) State the relative atomic mass of potassium. **(1 mark)**

Electron shells

The electrons in an atom are arranged in electron shells, or energy levels around the nucleus.

Filling the shells

You can work out the electronic configuration of an element from its atomic number. The electrons fill the shells that are closest to the nucleus first.

First (inner) shell - 2 electrons

Second shell - 8 electrons

Third shell - 8 electrons

Electronic configurations

The diagram shows the electronic configuration of sodium. This can also be written in numbers: 2.8.1

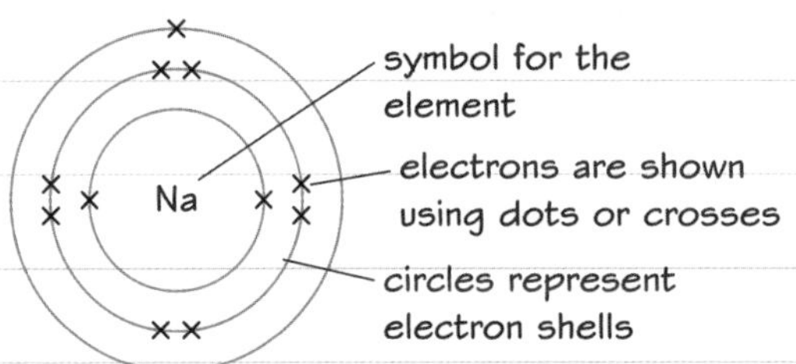
Na
symbol for the element
electrons are shown using dots or crosses
circles represent electron shells

Worked example

The atomic number of potassium is 19. Explain how its electrons are arranged.

An atom has the same number of protons and electrons, so a potassium atom has 19 electrons. The inner shell fills up first, and this shell is full when it has 2 electrons. The second shell has 8 electrons, and this is also full. This leaves 9 electrons. The third shell can hold 8 electrons, so that is full as well. The last shell has 1 electron in it. We write this as 2.8.8.1.

You do not need to learn the electronic configurations of any of the elements. But if you are told the atomic number of an element you need to be able to work out the electronic configuration.

Electrons and groups

1	2	3	4	5	6	7	0
H							He
Li	Be	B	C	N	O	F	Ne
Na	Mg	Al	Si	P	S	Cl	Ar
K	Ca						

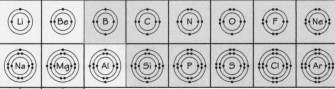

The group numbers are the same as the number of electrons in the outer shells (apartfrom group 0, where the outer shells are full).

The number of occupied shells is the same as the period number.

Now try this

target D-C
target G-E

1. Draw diagrams to show the electron arrangements in lithium and oxygen. **(4 marks)**
2. Sulfur is in group 6 of the periodic table. Explain how you can work out the number of outer electrons in a sulfur atom without knowing its atomic number. **(2 marks)**

Ions

Atoms and ions

An atom has the same number of protons and electrons. It has no overall charge, because the positive charges on the protons are balanced by the negative charges on the electrons.

An atom can become an ion by gaining or losing one or more electrons. An ion has a charge because it no longer has the same number of protons and electrons. We show that the atom has become an ion by adding a + or – sign to the symbol.

Cations

Metal atoms lose electrons to form positively charged cations.

- Metals in group 1 lose 1 electron to form ions with a 1+ charge.
- Metals in group 2 lose 2 electrons to form ions with a 2+ charge.

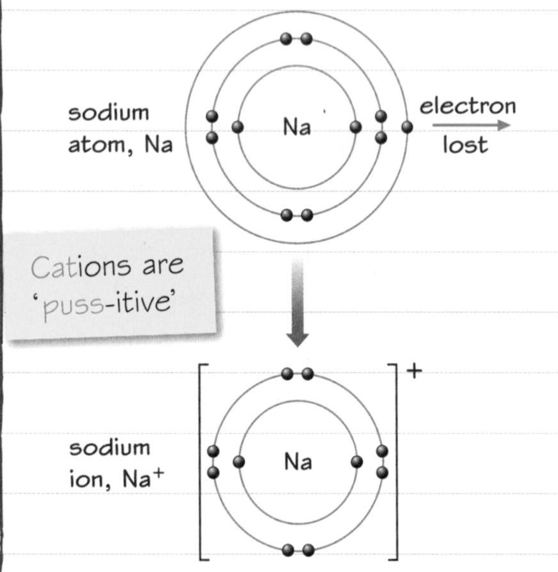

Cations are 'puss-itive'

Anions

Non-metal atoms (or groups of atoms) gain electrons to form negatively charged anions.

- Elements in group 6 gain 2 electrons to form ions with a 2– charge.
- Elements in group 7 gain 1 electron to form ions with a 1– charge.

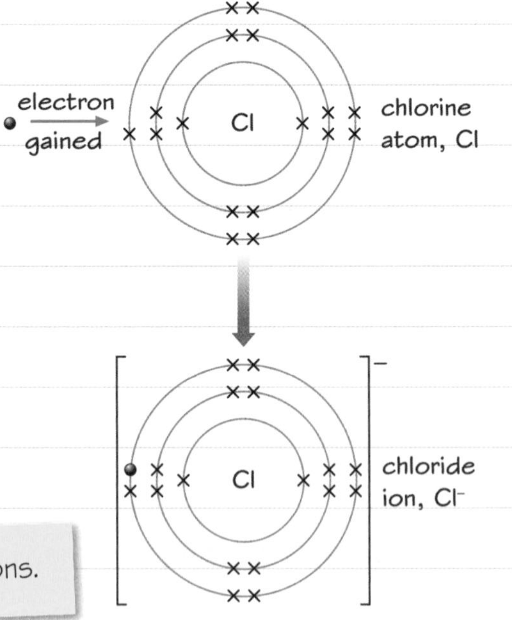

Non-metal atoms form Negative ions.

Now try this

1. State the type of element that forms:
   (a) anions **(1 mark)**
   (b) cations. **(1 mark)**

2. Write down the ions formed by the following elements. You may need to look at the periodic table on page 38 to help you.
   (a) calcium (Ca) **(1 mark)**
   (b) fluorine (F). **(1 mark)**

Ionic compounds

When sodium and chlorine react, sodium atoms lose electrons and chlorine atoms gain electrons. The sodium and chlorine ions have opposite charges, and they attract each other. This creates ionic bonds between the ions and a compound is formed. An ionic compound formed between a metal and a non-metal is called a salt.

Compound ions

Some groups of atoms can form ions. These are called compound ions.

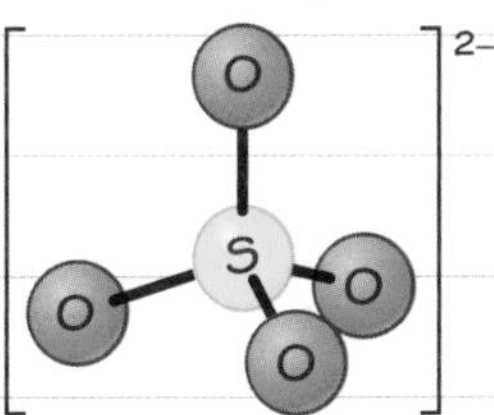

sulphate ion SO_4^{2-}

Some other compound ions are: hydroxide (OH^-), nitrate (NO_3^-) and carbonate (CO_3^{2+}).

The name of a compound tells you about the elements in it – so sodium chloride contains sodium and chlorine in the form of ions.

If the name of a compound ends in '-ate' it shows that oxygen is part of the compound as well. For example calcium carbonate contains calcium, carbon and oxygen.

A name ending in '-ide' shows that no extra oxygen is present. For example, copper sulfide contains only copper and sulfur. (Sodium hydroxide contains oxygen, but the 'ox' part of the name tells you that.)

Finding the formula

You need to be able to work out the formula of a compound if you are given the ions and their charges. The key thing is to remember that all the charges must cancel out.

calcium sulphide

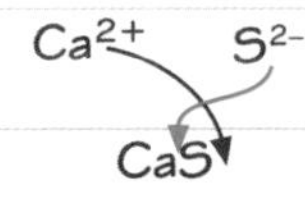

sodium oxide

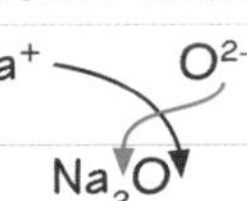

copper nitrate

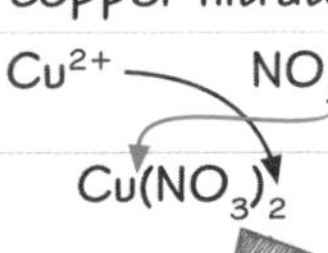

aluminium oxide

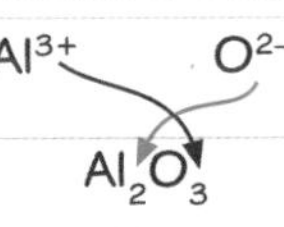

The nitrate ion is a compound ion. Use brackets if you need to put a number with a compound ion (e.g. magnesium hydroxide is $Mg(OH)_2$). If there is only one compound ion in a formula you do not need the brackets (e.g calcium carbonate is $CaCO_3$).

Easy method:

- Swap the numbers that give the charge for each ion and write them behind the relevant symbol.
- If the number is 1, don't write it in the formula.
- If both the numbers are the same, don't write them in the formula.

Now try this

1. Explain which of these compounds contain oxygen: calcium chloride, copper carbonate, potassium hydroxide, sodium sulfide, sodium sulfate. **(4 marks)**

target D-C

2. Write down the formulae of the compounds formed from:
   (a) calcium ions (Ca^{2+}) and sulfide ions (S^{2-}) **(1 mark)**
   (b) magnesium ions (Mg^{2+}) and nitrate ions (NO_3^-) **(1 mark)**
   (b) potassium ions (K^+) and sulfate ions (SO_4^{2-}). **(1 mark)**

Properties of ionic compounds

Melting and boiling points

Ionic substances have high melting points and high boiling points. This means they are solids at room temperature and have to be heated strongly to make them melt.

The melting point is the temperature at which a substance changes from a solid to a liquid (or when it changes from a liquid to a solid as it cools down). The boiling point is the temperature at which it changes from a liquid to a gas at the fastest possible rate.

Conducting electricity

Ionic substances *do not* conduct electricity when they are solid. They *do* conduct electricity when they are molten or dissolved in water ('in aqueous solution').

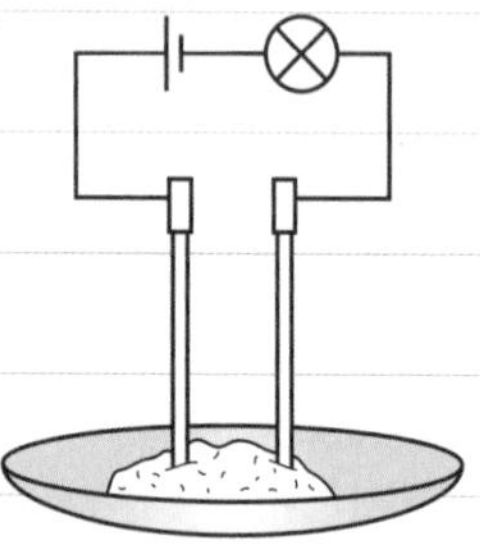
solid – does not conduct

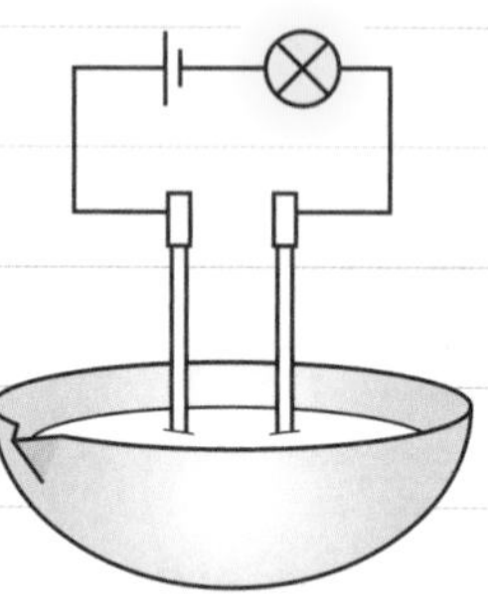
molten – conducts

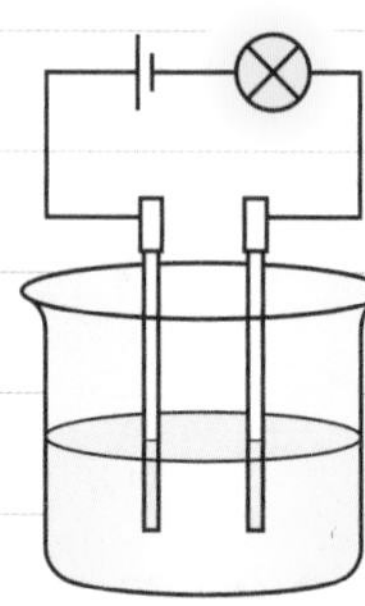
dissolved – conducts

Solubility rules

Many ionic substances dissolve in water. You need to learn the rules that help you to work out whether a particular substance is soluble.

If you can remember this rule it will help you to remember which carbonates and hydroxides *do* dissolve.

Soluble in water	Exceptions (insoluble in water)
all common salts of • sodium • potassium • ammonium	
all nitrates	
most chlorides	silver chloride, lead chloride
most sulfates	lead sulfate, barium sulfate, calcium sulfate

Insoluble in water	Exceptions (soluble in water)
most carbonates	sodium carbonate potassium carbonate ammonium carbonate
most hydroxides	sodium hydroxide potassium hydroxide ammonium hydroxide

There are no short cuts here – you just need to *learn* all of these rules.

Now try this

1. State which of these ionic substances will conduct electricity:
   (a) molten barium sulfate **(1 mark)**
   (b) copper sulfate powder **(1 mark)**
   (c) sodium chloride solution. **(1 mark)**

2. State whether each of these substances is soluble or insoluble in water:
   (a) barium sulfate **(1 mark)**
   (b) copper sulfate **(1 mark)**
   (c) calcium carbonate. **(1 mark)**

Precipitates

If you mix solutions of two soluble salts, the ions in the mixture can combine to form new salts. If one of the new combinations produces an insoluble salt, it will appear as a precipitate. You can use the solubility rules to work out if a precipitate will form.

Predicting precipitates

Worked example

Silver nitrate solution is mixed with potassium chloride solution. Explain why a precipitate will form and write equations for the reaction.

Silver chloride is insoluble, so when silver and chloride ions come into contact they will form a precipitate.

silver nitrate + potassium chloride → silver chloride + potassium nitrate

$AgNO_3(aq) + KCl(aq) \rightarrow AgCl(s) + KNO_3(aq)$

The letters in brackets tell you the state of each substance.

(s) = solid, (l) = liquid, (g) = gas, (aq) = aqueous (dissolved in water)

EXAM ALERT!

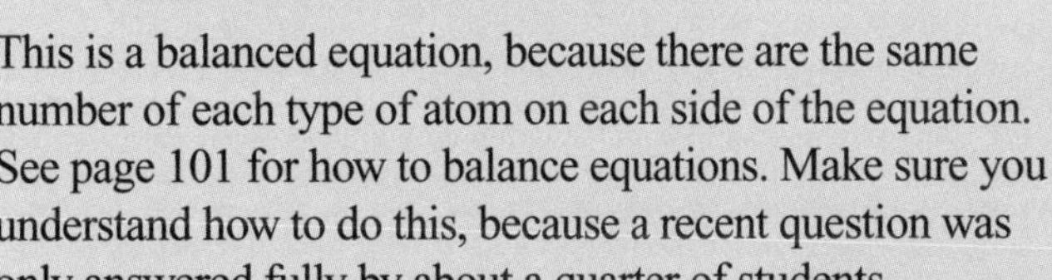

This is a balanced equation, because there are the same number of each type of atom on each side of the equation. See page 101 for how to balance equations. Make sure you understand how to do this, because a recent question was only answered fully by about a quarter of students.

Students have struggled with exam questions similar to this - **be prepared!**

Preparing salts

Pure samples of insoluble salts can be prepared using precipitation reactions.

Mix solutions of two soluble substances that will form the insoluble salt. → Filter the mixture. The insoluble salt will be trapped in the filter paper. → Wash the salt with pure water. → Leave the salt to dry on the filter paper. It could be dried in an oven.

Barium sulfate

Barium sulfate is an insoluble salt. It is given as a 'barium meal' to patients who are going to have their stomachs or intestines X-rayed because:

- barium sulfate is opaque to X-rays, so it shows up well on the X-ray picture.
- it is safe to use (barium salts are toxic, but because barium sulfate is insoluble barium does not get into the patient's blood).

Now try this

1. Explain what will happen when these substances are mixed:
   (a) sodium carbonate and calcium nitrate **(3 marks)**
   (b) potassium nitrate and ammonium carbonate. **(2 marks)**

Ion tests

Some of the ions in salts can be identified using tests in the laboratory.

Flame tests

Some metal ions can be identified using flame tests. A damp splint is placed in the solid and then held in a Bunsen burner flame. The colour of the flame identifies the ions.

Metal ion	Flame test colour
sodium (Na^+)	yellow
potassium (K^+)	lilac
calcium (Ca^{2+})	red-yellow
copper (Cu^{2+})	green-blue

Spectroscopy

Worked example

Describe how a spectroscope was used to discover new elements.

Very small amounts of some elements can be detected in flame tests by using a spectroscope. The elements rubidium and caesium were discovered when scientists spotted colours in parts of the spectrum they had not seen before.

Test for carbonate ions (CO_3^{2-})

- Add dilute acid to the substance.
- Test the gas given off with limewater.

If the substance contains carbonate ions:

- it will fizz or bubble as a gas is given off
- the gas will turn limewater milky, showing the gas is carbon dioxide.

Test for sulfate ions (SO_4^{2-})

- Add a few drops of dilute hydrochloric acid.
- Shake the mixture.
- Add a few drops of barium chloride solution.

If the substance contains sulfate ions:

- a white precipitate of barium sulfate forms.

Test for chloride ions (Cl^-)

- Add a few drops of dilute nitric acid to the solution.
- Shake the mixture.
- Add a few drops of silver nitrate solution.

If the substance contains chloride ions:

- a white precipitate of silver chloride forms.

EXAM ALERT!

If you are asked to describe the test for a substance, you need to say how to carry out the test *and* what you would see if the substance is the one you expect.

Students have struggled with exam questions similar to this - **be prepared!**

Now try this

1. State which ions give these flame colours:
   (a) red **(1 mark)**
   (b) lilac. **(1 mark)**

2. A student uses these substances to test an unknown compound. State which ions each substance is used to test for:
   (a) silver nitrate **(1 mark)**
   (b) limewater **(1 mark)**
   (c) barium chloride. **(1 mark)**

Chemistry extended writing 1

When answering extended writing questions you should try to:

- ✓ Apply your scientific knowledge.
- ✓ Present your answer in a logical and organised way.
- ✓ Write a full answer and make sure that your spelling, punctuation and grammar are as good as you can make them.

Worked example

Fluorine has a mass number of 19 and an atomic number of 9.
Describe the numbers and arrangements of the protons, neutrons and electrons in an atom of fluorine. **(6 marks)**

Sample answer 1

The atomic number is the number of protons and the mass number is the number of neutrons and they are in the middle of the atom and the electrons are around the outside.

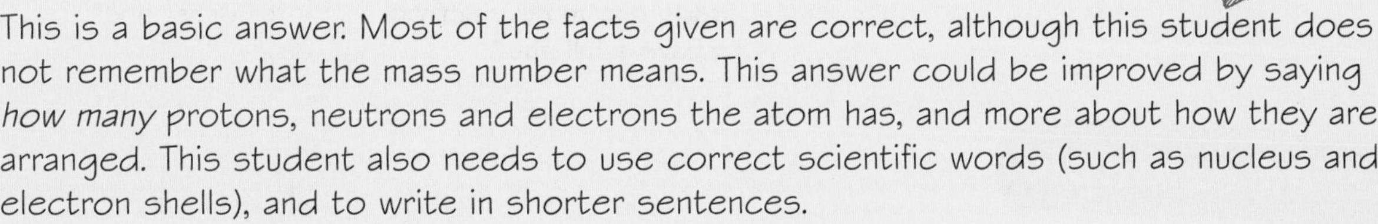
This is a basic answer. Most of the facts given are correct, although this student does not remember what the mass number means. This answer could be improved by saying *how many* protons, neutrons and electrons the atom has, and more about how they are arranged. This student also needs to use correct scientific words (such as nucleus and electron shells), and to write in shorter sentences.

Sample answer 2

The atomic number shows that fluorine has 9 protons in the nucleus. The mass number is the total number of protons and neutrons, so fluorine has 10 neutrons. These are also in the nucleus.

An atom always has the same number of protons and electrons, so a fluorine atom has 9 electrons. These are arranged in shells around the nucleus. The first shell holds 2 electrons and the second one can hold up to 8. There are only 7 electrons left after two of them have gone into the first shell, so the electronic configuration of fluorine is 2.7.

This is an excellent, detailed answer. As well as giving all the details about the structure of the atom and the numbers of different particles, this answer also uses scientific words and phrases correctly (such as 'electronic configuration'). It is also written in sentences and paragraphs with correct spelling and grammar.

Now try this

1. The electronic configuration of calcium is 2.8.8.2. The electronic configuration of oxygen is 2.6. Explain what these configurations tell you about atoms of these elements and how they will react together. **(6 marks)**

Covalent bonds

Molecules consist of two or more atoms chemically joined together. The atoms are held together by covalent bonds. A covalent bond is a pair of electrons that is shared between two atoms.

In all kinds of bonding, atoms lose, gain or share electrons to get a full outer shell. Covalent bonding takes place between non-metal atoms. Non-metal atoms need one or more electrons to fill their outer shell, and they do this by sharing the electrons.

Dot and cross diagrams

We can show the formation of simple, molecular covalent substances using dot and cross diagrams.

The electrons in the atoms are all the same. We use dots and crosses to help us see which electrons came from the different atoms.

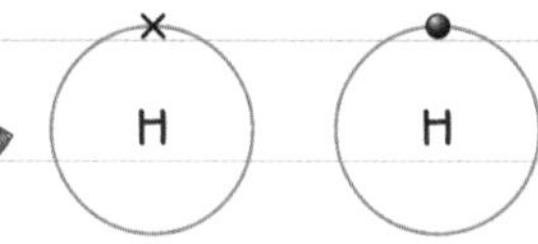

Hydrogen atoms each have one electron. The first shell can hold two electrons, so each atom needs one more electron to have a full shell.

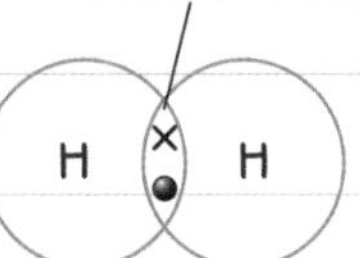

A hydrogen molecule has two hydrogen atoms sharing their electrons. Both atoms now have a full outer shell.

Worked example

Draw dot and cross diagrams to show the covalent bonds in:

(a) hydrogen chloride (HCl) **(b)** water (H_2O) **(c)** methane (CH_4).

a)

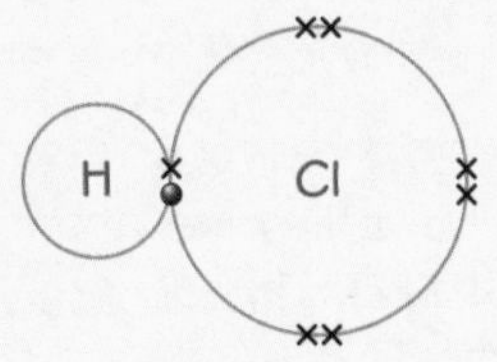

b)

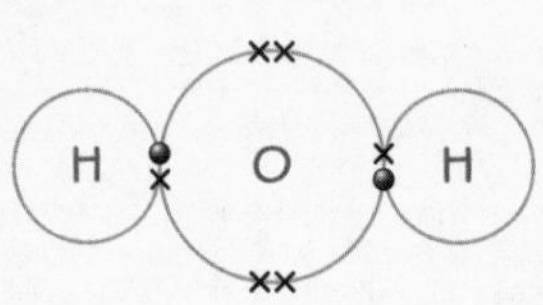

c)

The diagram only shows the outer electron shells for each atom, as these are the ones involved in the bonds. Look back at page 39 to remind yourself about the arrangement of electrons in atoms.

Now try this

1. Which of the following types of atoms form covalent bonds when they join together? **(1 mark)**

A two metal atoms

B two non-metal atoms

C a metal and a non-metal atom

2. The electronic configuration of carbon is 2.4.

(a) State how many electrons a carbon atom needs to fill its outer shell. **(1 mark)**

(b) Explain why the formula of methane is CH_4. **(3 marks)**

Covalent substances

Substances with covalent bonds can form small molecules or giant structures. The two types of substances have different properties.

Simple molecular covalent substances

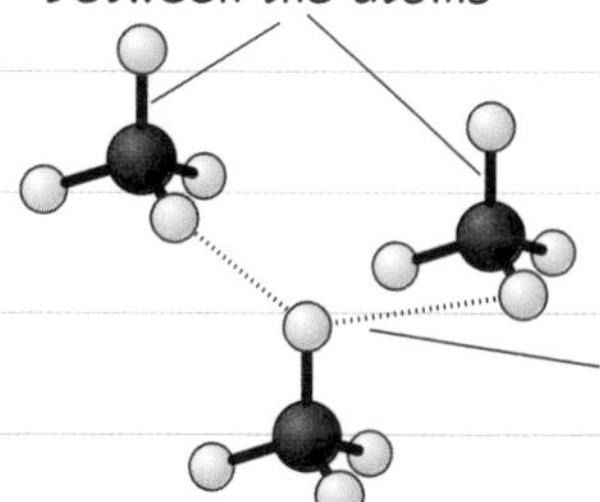

Many simple molecular covalent substances are liquids or gases at room temperature so weak forces between the molecules substances have low melting points and low boiling points

There are no charged particles, so simple molecular covalent substances do not conduct electricity.

Giant molecular covalent substances

Diamond is a giant molecular covalent substance and is made of billions of atoms all joined.

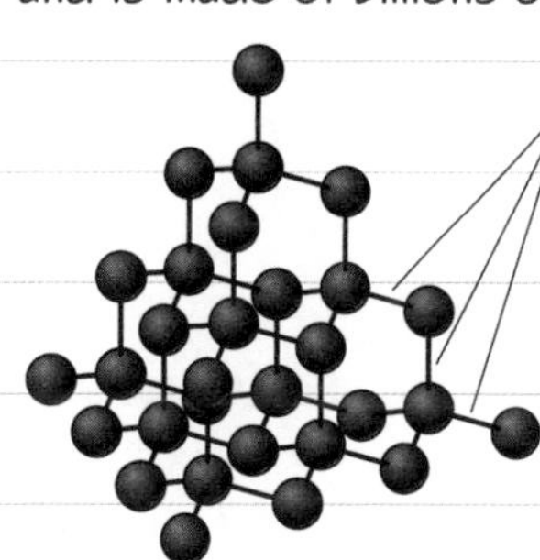

The covalent bonds in giant molecular covalent substances are strong. It takes a lot of energy to break these bonds so melting points and boiling points are very high. These substances are very hard and do not conduct electricity.

Worked example

Complete the table to summarise the differences between different covalent substances.

Property	Simple molecular covalent substances	Most giant molecular covalent substances, including diamond	Graphite
Melting and boiling points	low	high	high
State at room temperature	liquids or gases, or solids with low melting points such as sugar or wax	solids	solid
Conduct electricity?	no	no	yes
Hardness	–	hard	soft

Graphite

Graphite is also a giant molecular covalent substance, so it has a high melting point, but some of its properties are different from diamond. It does conduct electricity and is very soft.

EXAM ALERT!

A recent exam question on this topic was only fully answered by around a quarter of students. Remember, in simple molecular substances the bonds between the molecules are weak but the bonds between the atoms are strong.

Students have struggled with this topic in recent exams - **be prepared!** ResultsPlus

Now try this

1. Ethane is a simple molecular covalent compound. Explain why it is a gas at room temperature. **(2 marks)**
2. Sand (silicon dioxide) is made of silicon and oxygen atoms joined in a giant structure. Explain why:
   (a) grains of sand are hard **(1 mark)**
   (b) sand does not conduct electricity **(1 mark)**
   (c) sand is a solid at room temperature. **(2 marks)**

Miscible or immiscible?

Miscible liquids mix completely with each other. Immiscible liquids do not mix completely.

Separating immiscible liquids

Worked example

The diagram shows a separating funnel. Explain how this can be used to separate two immiscible liquids.

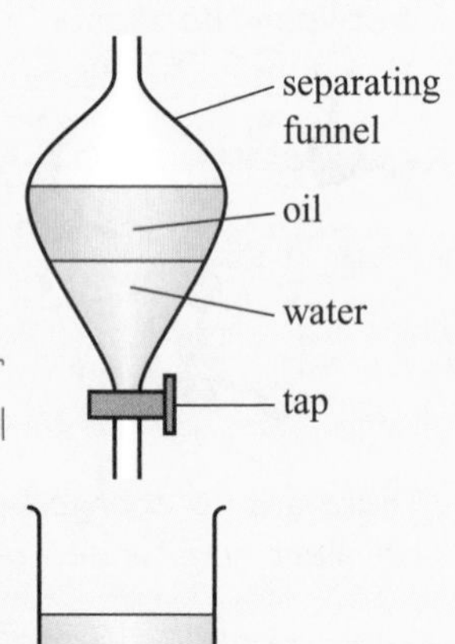

Place the mixture in the funnel and put a beaker underneath. Open the tap until most of the lower liquid has run into the beaker. Put a clean beaker under the funnel and run the last bit of the lower liquid and a little bit from the top liquid into the beaker. Place a final clean beaker under the tap and run off all of the second liquid.

The liquid with the lowest density is at the top. In this example, you can see that oil is less dense than water.

Separating miscible liquids

Miscible liquids can be separated using fractional distillation.

- The mixture is heated, and the vapours pass into a fractionating column.
- As the gases cool down, the ones with the highest boiling points condense first.
- Different liquids are collected at different places in the column.

Fractional distillation only works if the two liquids in the mixture have different boiling points.

Distillation of liquid air

Nitrogen and oxygen are obtained from air by fractional distillation. The air has to be turned to a liquid first by cooling it.

Remember: −190°C is colder than −185°C.

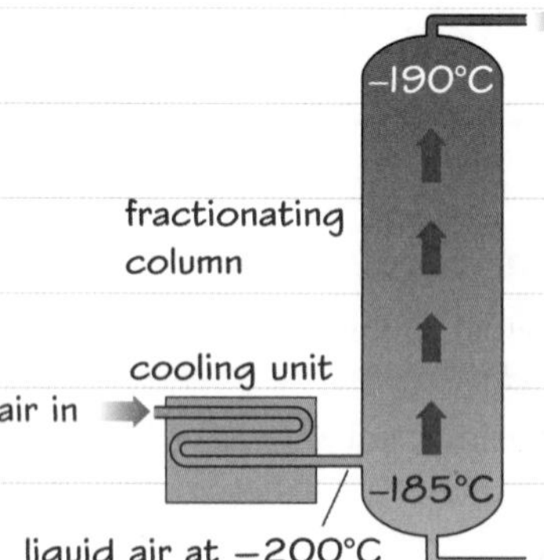

nitrogen gas is collected

−185 °C is above the boiling point of nitrogen and so the nitrogen boils and evaporates.

−185 °C is below the boiling point of oxygen and a lot of the oxygen stays as a liquid (although some evaporates).

liquid oxygen piped out

Now try this

1. Oil and water form separate layers when they are shaken together. Ethanol and water mix completely.
   - **(a)** State which mixture is miscible. **(1 mark)**
   - **(b)** Name the process you would use to separate the miscible mixture. **(2 marks)**

2. Salad dressing is a mixture of oil and vinegar. Oil and vinegar are immiscible liquids. Explain why a bottle of salad dressing needs to be shaken before it is used. **(2 marks)**

Chromatography

Most inks, paints, dyes and food colourings are mixtures of different coloured compounds. Chromatography can be used to separate the different substances in these mixtures.

If you are asked to draw the apparatus for chromatography, make sure the line for the solvent is above the bottom edge of the paper but below the samples. If the samples are dipped into the solvent they will just dissolve into it.

Paper chromatography

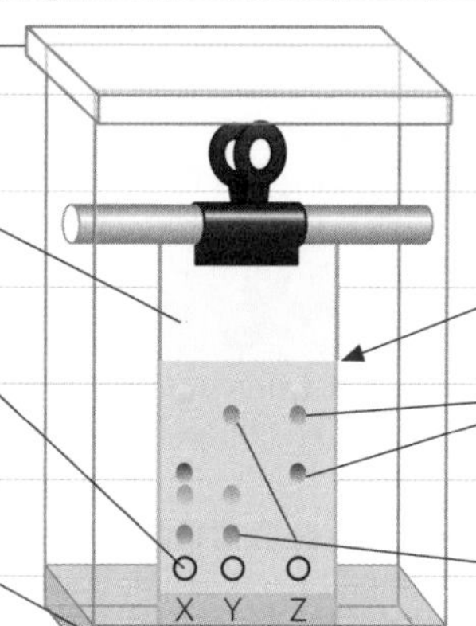

lid (to stop evaporation of solvent)

Drops of the different samples are put onto the paper and allowed to dry. The bottom of the paper is then dipped into a solvent.
Solvent (this can be water or some other liquid that the samples will dissolve in)

Solvent front (the solvent has reached this level)

More soluble compounds are carried up the paper faster than less soluble ones, so the compounds separate out.

R_f values

The R_f value of a compound is always the same as long as the chromatography is carried out in the same way, under the same conditions. R_f values can be used to identify compounds from a chromatogram.

$$R_f = \frac{\text{distance moved by compound}}{\text{distance moved by solvent}}$$

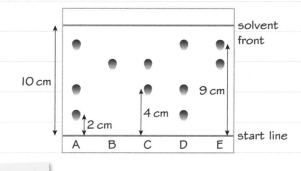

solvent front
10 cm
2 cm
4 cm
9 cm
start line
A B C D E

R_f is one distance divided by another, so it has no units.

Worked example

Calculate the R_f value for the lowest spot for sample A on the chromatogram above.

$$R_f = \frac{2\text{ cm}}{10\text{ cm}} = 0.2$$

A compound never gets as far up the paper as the solvent, so the R_f value must always be less than 1.

Chromatography can be used...

- in the food industry, to check which colourings are used in food
- in forensic science, to analyse DNA samples or paints and inks from crime scenes
- by museums to analyse paints, to help them to restore old paintings or detect forgeries.

Now try this

1. In the chromatogram illustration above, which of the samples:
   (a) contains the same dyes as sample A? **(1 mark)**
   (b) contains only one dye? **(1 mark)**
   (c) contain two dyes? **(1 mark)**

2. (a) Calculate the R_f value for the lowest spot for sample C. **(2 marks)**
   (b) Which spot (or spots) have an R_f value of 0.9? **(1 mark)**

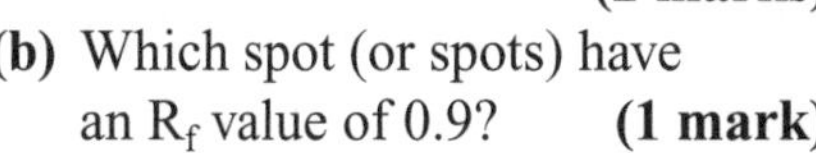

Chemical classification 1

Elements and compounds can be classified into different types.

Ionic substances

Bonding:
- atoms gain or lose electrons to form ions
- strong bonds between ions

Electricity:
- conduct electricity when molten or dissolved in water
- do not conduct when solid

sodium chloride

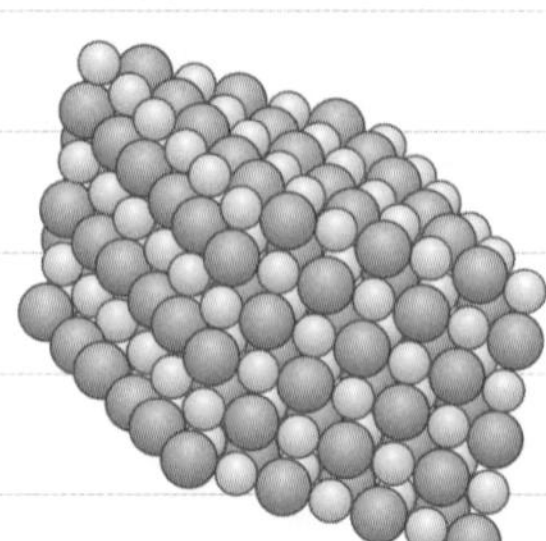

Melting and boiling points:
- high
- ionic substances are solids at room temperature

Solubility:
- many dissolve in water

Simple molecular covalent substances

Bonding:
- atoms share electrons to get a full outer shell
- strong bonds between atoms in molecules
- weak forces between separate molecules

Electricity:
- do not conduct electricity

water, oxygen

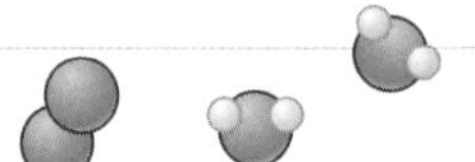

Melting and boiling points:
- low
- most simple molecular covalent substances are liquids or gases at room temperature

Solubility:
- some dissolve in water

Giant molecular covalent substances

Bonding:
- atoms share electrons to get a full outer shell
- strong bonds between all the atoms in a structure

Electricity:
- do not conduct electricity (except for graphite)

sand (silicon dioxide)

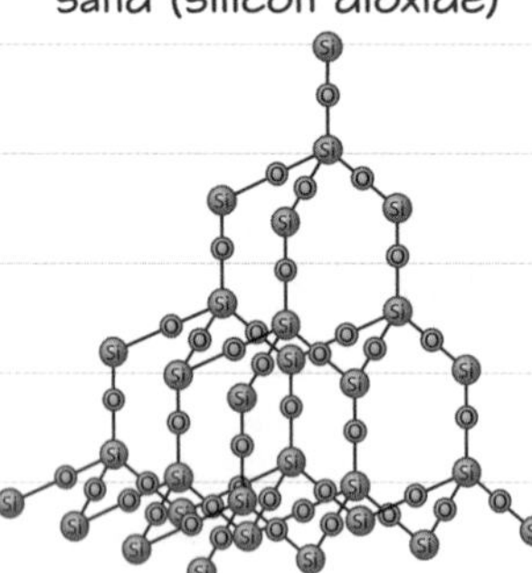

Melting and boiling points:
- high
- giant molecular covalent substances are solids at room temperature

Solubility:
- insoluble (do not dissolve in water)

Now try this

target G-E

1. List the types of substances that:
   (a) never conduct electricity **(1 mark)**
   (b) are always solids at room temperature **(1 mark)**
   (c) form structures made from millions of atoms. **(1 mark)**

target E-C

2. Describe the similarities and differences between ionic and covalent bonding. **(2 marks)**

Chemical classification 2

Elements and compounds can be classified into different types.

Metals

Bonding:
- positive ions held together by a sea of delocalised electrons
- strength of bonds is stronger in some metals than others

Electricity:
- conduct electricity when solid and liquid

any metal

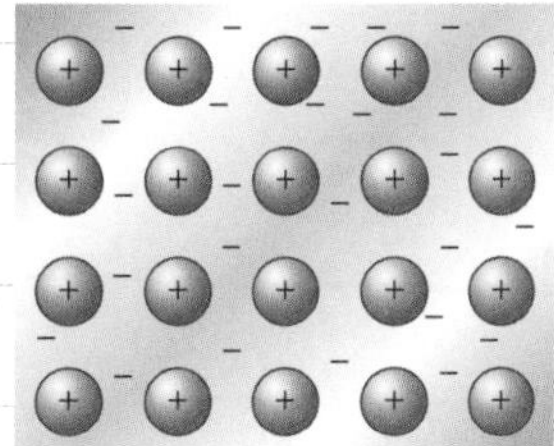

Melting and boiling points:
- medium to high
- all metals except mercury are solids at room temperature

Solubility:
- insoluble (do not dissolve in water)

Classifying substances

You can carry out simple tests on substances to help you classify them into ionic substances, metals, simple molecular covalent substances and giant molecular covalent substances.

Melting point:
- If a substance is a liquid it is probably a simple molecular covalent substance, because these are usually liquids or gases at room temperature.
- If the substance is a solid, put some of it in a crucible and heat it using a Bunsen burner.
- If the substance melts easily it is probably simple molecular covalent. Most metals and giant covalent substances have very high melting points and many giant ionic substances cannot be melted with the Bunsen burner.

Conducting electricity: Use a battery, bulb and some wires to see if the substance conducts electricity.
- If it conducts electricity when it is solid it is a metal (or graphite).
- If it does not conduct when it is solid, try dissolving it in water. If it dissolves and the solution *does* conduct electricity, then it is an ionic substance.

Worked example

How can you use the solubility of a substance to help you to classify it?

I can test the substance to see if it dissolves in water. If it does dissolve it could be an ionic substance, or a simple molecular covalent substance. If it does not dissolve, it does not show that it is *not* one of these substances, as not all ionic or simple molecular covalent substances are soluble.

When you are describing tests, be sure to say what results you may get and what these results mean.

You need to use the results of all the different tests for a substance to help you to decide how to classify it.

Now try this

1. You test a solid substance at room temperature, and find that it conducts electricity. Explain why this test shows that the substance is a metal and not an ionic substance. **(2 marks)**
2. You have a sample of a substance that dissolves in water.
   (a) Explain which two types of substances this sample could belong to. **(2 marks)**
   (b) Explain how you would use a cell and electrodes to find out whether it is an ionic substance or a simple molecular covalent substance. **(2 marks)**

Metals and bonding

Metals are malleable and can conduct electricity. To understand why you need to know about the bonding in them.

Metallic bonding

A metal consists of a regular arrangement of positive ions surrounded by a 'sea' of delocalised electrons. These electrons come from the outer shells of the atoms and can move around throughout the metal.

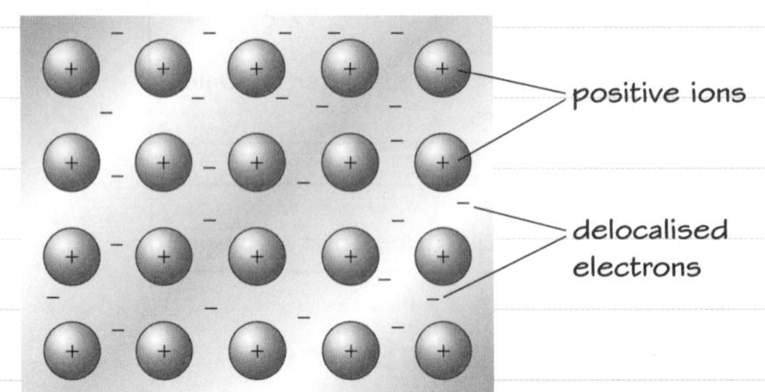

Worked example

How does the arrangement of ions in a solid metal explain its properties?

You will only be asked to explain why metals conduct electricity and why they are malleable (can be hammered into different shapes without breaking).

Metals conduct electricity because the delocalised electrons can move through the metal. When there is a potential difference across a piece of metal, the delocalised electrons drift in one direction to form an electric current.

Metals are malleable because the layers of positive ions can slide over each other if a force is applied to the metal.

Transition metals

Transition metals are the metals in the central block of the periodic table. Most metals are transition metals.

Transition metals typically:

- have high melting points
- form coloured compounds.

Be careful not to say that transition metals 'are coloured' or 'form colours'.

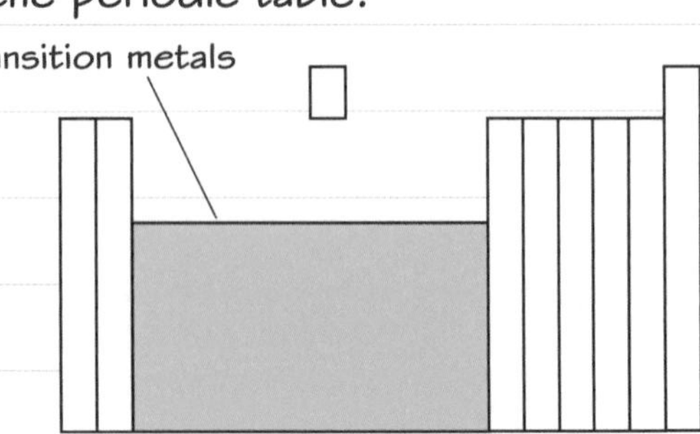

Now try this

1. Describe the arrangement of ions and electrons in a metal. **(2 marks)**

2. (a) State the meaning of malleable. **(1 mark)**
   (b) Explain why metals are malleable. **(2 marks)**

Alkali metals

Properties

The alkali metals are in group 1 of the periodic table. The alkali metals:

- are soft metals (you can cut them with a knife)
- have comparatively low melting points (they are easy to melt).

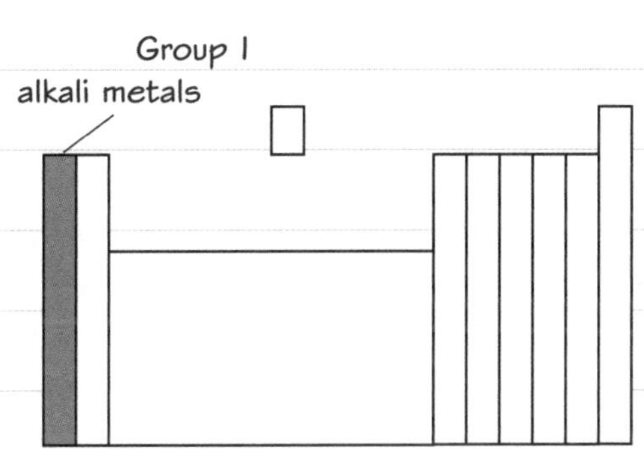

Reactions with water

The alkali metals are all in the same group of the periodic table so they all have similar reactions. They all have one electron in the outer shell, so when they react, each atom loses one electron to become an ion with a +1 charge.

All the alkali metals react with water to form a metal hydroxide and hydrogen gas. Metal hydroxides are alkaline.

lithium + water → lithium hydroxide + hydrogen

$2Li(s) + 2H_2O(l) \rightarrow 2LiOH(aq) + H_2(g)$

You may be asked to write balanced equations for this reaction, or for the reactions of sodium or potassium. The formulae for the other hydroxides are similar, because the alkali metals all form ions with a charge of +1. The other hydroxides are NaOH and KOH.

Reactivity

The reactivity of the alkali metals increases down the group. When they are put in water:

- lithium floats on the surface and fizzes
- sodium melts from the heat produced by the reaction and whizzes around on the surface as a molten ball, and sometimes the hydrogen produced catches fire
- potassium reacts even faster, and the hydrogen produced burns with a lilac flame.

Worked example

Rubidium is an alkali metal below potassium in group 1 of the periodic table. Explain how reactive this metal is compared to potassium.

The reactivity of the alkali metals increases as you go down the table, so sodium is more reactive than lithium, and potassium is more reactive than sodium. As rubidium is below potassium, it will be more reactive than potassium.

Now try this

1. Suggest why experiments with rubidium are not allowed in school laboratories. **(2 marks)**

2. Write a balanced equation for the reaction of sodium with water. Include state symbols. **(3 marks)**

Halogens

Group 7

The halogens are the elements in group 7 of the periodic table. They have similar reactions to each other because if they can gain one electron they can each complete their outer shell. They all react with metals to form compounds called halides. Fluorine is the most reactive halogen, and the reactivity decreases as you go down the group.

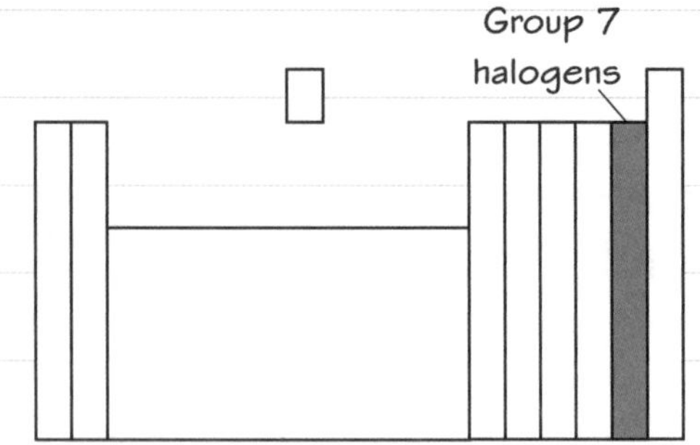

Properties of halogens

Element	Symbol	State at room temperature	Colour
fluorine	F	gas	pale yellow
chlorine	Cl	gas	yellow-green
bromine	Br	liquid	red-brown
iodine	I	solid	grey

You need to learn the states and colours of the halogens.

The symbols in the table are for atoms of the halogens. The halogens form molecules with two atoms in them, so the formulae for the halogens at room temperature are $F_2(g)$, $Cl_2(g)$, $Br_2(l)$ and $I_2(s)$.

Worked example

All the halogens react with metals to form compounds called halides. Write word equations and balanced equations to show the reactions between:

(a) potassium and chlorine **(b)** calcium and bromine.

(a) potassium + chlorine → potassium chloride

$2K(s) + Cl_2(g) \rightarrow 2KCl(s)$

(b) calcium + bromine → calcium bromide

$Ca(s) + Br_2(l) \rightarrow CaBr_2(s)$

You may be asked to write balanced equations for the reactions of any of the halogens with metals. There is more about balancing equations on page 101.

Now try this

1. Chlorine and bromine will both react with sodium. Explain which reaction will occur more quickly. **(2 marks)**
2. Write a word equation and a balanced equation to show the reaction between sodium (Na) and bromine. The formula of sodium bromide is NaBr. **(3 marks)**

More halogen reactions

Reactions with hydrogen

Halogens react with hydrogen to form hydrogen halides. Hydrogen halides dissolve in water to form acidic solutions. For example, when hydrogen chloride is dissolved in water it forms hydrochloric acid.

hydrogen + chlorine → hydrogen chloride

$H_2(g) + Cl_2(g) \rightarrow 2HCl(g)$

All halogens need one electron to complete their outer shell. The formulae for the other hydrogen halides are similar: HF, HBr, HI.

Displacement reactions

Some halogens will displace another halogen from a solution. The table shows how different combinations of halogens and halides react.

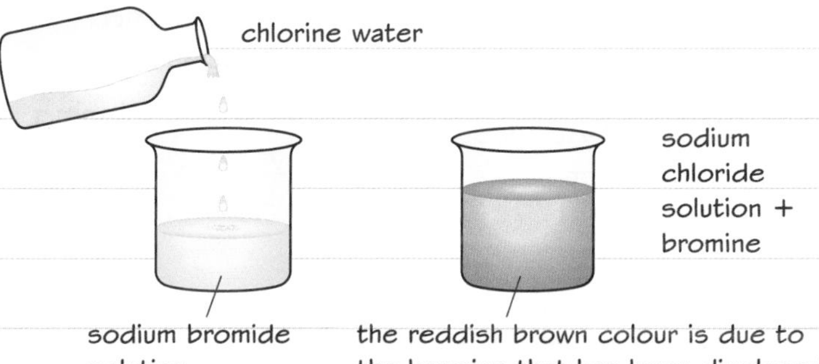

$2NaBr(aq) + Cl_2(aq) \rightarrow 2NaCl(aq) + Br_2(aq)$

halogen	halide ions: fluoride	chloride	bromide	iodide
fluorine		reaction	reaction	reaction
chlorine	no reaction		reaction	reaction
bromine	no reaction	no reaction		reaction
iodine	no reaction	no reaction	no reaction	

Worked example

The table above shows the results of mixing different halogens with solutions containing different halide ions. Explain these results using ideas about reactivity.

Remember that the most reactive halogen is at the *top* of the group. This is the opposite way round to the alkali metals, where the most reactive elements are at the *bottom*.

Fluorine is the most reactive halogen, and the reactivity decreases as you go down the group. Because fluorine is more reactive, it will displace any of the other halogens from their compounds.

Chlorine is less reactive than fluorine, but more reactive than bromine or iodine. If chlorine is mixed with a fluoride solution it will not react, but chlorine will displace bromide or iodide ions from their solutions.

Now try this

1. Write the formula for hydrochloric acid, including a state symbol. **(2 marks)**

2. Write a word equation and balanced equation to show the reaction between hydrogen and bromine. **(4 marks)**

Noble gases

The noble gases are the elements in group 0 of the periodic table. They all have a full outer electron shell. This is the most stable arrangement of electrons, which other elements only achieve by making ions or sharing electrons in covalent bonds. This is why the noble gases are inert, compared with other elements. This means it is very difficult to make them react.

Uses	Gas	Reason for use
welding	argon or helium	the gases are inert so they do not react with the hot metal, and they stop oxygen coming into contact with it
inside filament light bulbs	xenon or argon	the gases are inert so they do not react with the hot filament
balloons and airships	helium	helium has a low density and makes the balloons float
fire-extinguishing systems	argon	argon is non-flammable, so it can be used to put out fires

Discovery

Lord Rayleigh noticed that the density of nitrogen made in a reaction was lower than the density of nitrogen obtained from air.

Sir William Ramsey hypothesised that the air might also contain a denser gas that was mixed with the nitrogen.

Rayleigh and Ramsey carried out some careful experiments and discovered a new gas – argon.

During the experiments Ramsey also discovered helium. Later, he also discovered neon, krypton and xenon.

Worked example

The table shows the densities and boiling points of some of the noble gases. Describe the trends in these properties and use them to predict the missing numbers.

Element	Density (kg/m^3)	Boiling point (°C)
helium (He)	0.15	−269
neon (Ne)	1.20	
argon (Ar)		−186
krypton (Kr)	2.15	−152

The densities increase as you go down the group. The boiling points get higher as you go down the group.

The density of argon could be about 1.7 or 1.8 kg/m^3.

The boiling point of neon could be about −230 °C

These numbers are about halfway between the numbers above and below in the table.

You do need to be able to answer questions like this one that ask you to identify a trend, and use the trend to predict missing values.

Now try this

1. Xenon is a noble gas below krypton in group 0. Suggest what its density and boiling point could be. **(2 marks)**

2. Explain which properties are important for the following uses:
   (a) helium used in airships **(2 marks)**
   (b) argon used in welding. **(2 marks)**

Chemistry extended writing 2

Worked example

Sodium is an alkali metal. Copper is a transition metal.

Compare the similarities and differences of alkali metals and transition metals. **(6 marks)**

Sample answer 1

They are metals, they fizz with water. They make coloured compounds and they conduct electricity and they can be hammered.

This answer is not likely to gain any marks. If a question asks you to 'compare' two things or groups, you need to write about similarities and differences. Although some similarities between the two groups of metals are mentioned (they conduct electricity and they can be hammered), these are in the same sentence as a property that only applies to transition metals. When you are comparing two things, or two groups of things, it must be very clear which things you are writing about in each sentence.

Sample answer 2

They are all metals, so they all conduct electricity and they are all malleable.

Differences:

	Alkali metals	Transition metals
compounds	white compounds	many form coloured compounds
melting point	fairly low	high
hardness	soft	mostly hard
water	react with water and make hydrogen and alkali	

This is a very good answer. The similarities are given in the first sentence, and the differences are clearly presented in a table. The answer also uses correct scientific words for the properties, such as 'malleable'.

Now try this

1. Fluorine and bromine are elements in group 7 of the periodic table. They both react with hydrogen and with metals.
   Compare these elements and their reactions. **(6 marks)**

Chemistry extended writing 3

Worked example

The halogens are elements in group 7 of the periodic table. Explain how atoms of the halogens are held together in molecules and why the halogens have low melting and boiling points. **(6 marks)**

Sample answer 1

They have low points because they are all gases or liquids at room temperature. They all make compounds.

This is a very poor answer. Most of the facts are wrong.

For example, fluorine and chlorine are gases at room temperature, bromine is a liquid and iodine is a solid. Fluorine and chlorine are gases *because* they have low boiling points, not the other way round.

The statement that all the halogens can form compounds is correct, but does not answer the part of the question that is asking about the bonding between halogen atoms.

Sample answer 2

The elements in group 7 form molecules such as Cl_2 and Br_2. The atoms in each molecule are held together by sharing electrons in a covalent bond. These bonds are very strong. There are only weak forces between the separate molecules. When a solid melts, heat energy is used to pull the particles apart, so if the forces are weak then not much heat energy is needed and the solid melts at a low temperature. The same thing for boiling.

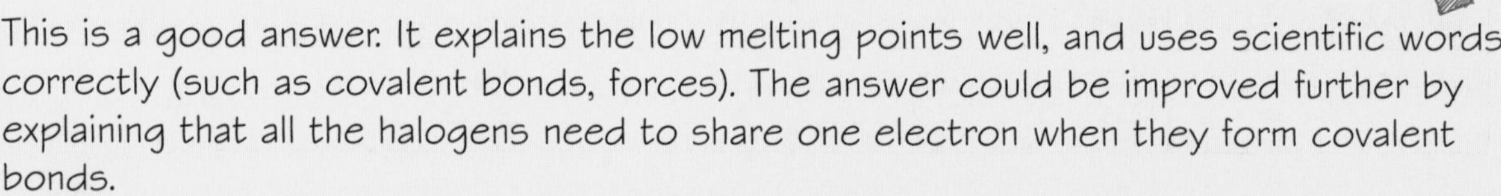

This is a good answer. It explains the low melting points well, and uses scientific words correctly (such as covalent bonds, forces). The answer could be improved further by explaining that all the halogens need to share one electron when they form covalent bonds.

Now try this

1. The diagrams show the structures of carbon dioxide (diagram a) and silicon dioxide (which forms sand and is diagram b).

   Explain the similarities and differences in the properties of these substances. Use the bonding and structures of the substances to help you.`

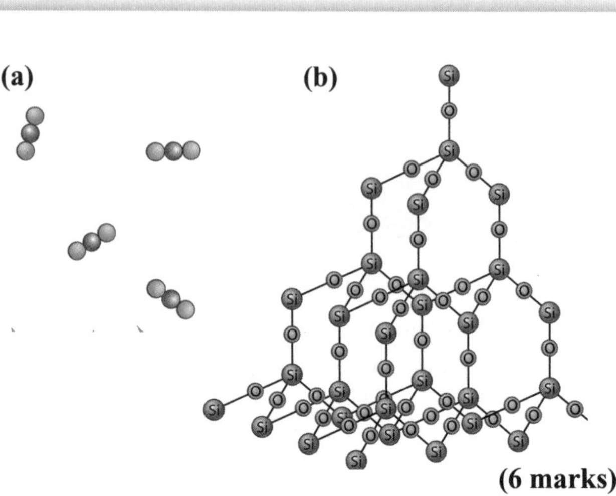

(6 marks)

Temperature changes

Temperature changes

Most reactions involve a temperature change.

- In exothermic reactions, heat energy is given out (the reaction mixture or the surroundings become hot).
- In endothermic reactions, heat energy is taken in (the reaction mixture gets cold).

EXAM ALERT!

A recent exam question on energy changes was only answered fully by about one-third of students. Remember: if the temperature increases, the reaction is exothermic. If the temperature decreases, the reaction is endothermic.

Students have struggled with this topic in recent exams - **be prepared!** ResultsPlus

Measuring temperature changes

You can use this apparatus to investigate temperature changes in reactions.

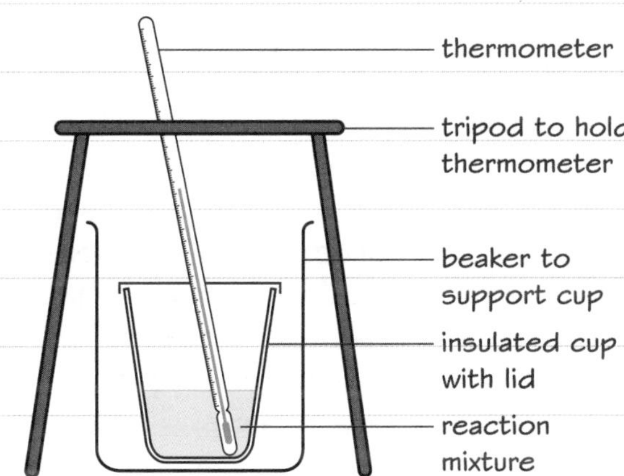

Bonds and energy

When a chemical reaction happens, the bonds that hold the atoms together in the molecules of the reactants are broken. The atoms then come together in new arrangements to form the products.

- Breaking bonds is endothermic (energy is needed).
- Making bonds is exothermic (energy is released).

Exothermic reaction
The energy given out when the products form is *greater than* the energy needed to break the bonds in the reactants. Overall, energy is given out.

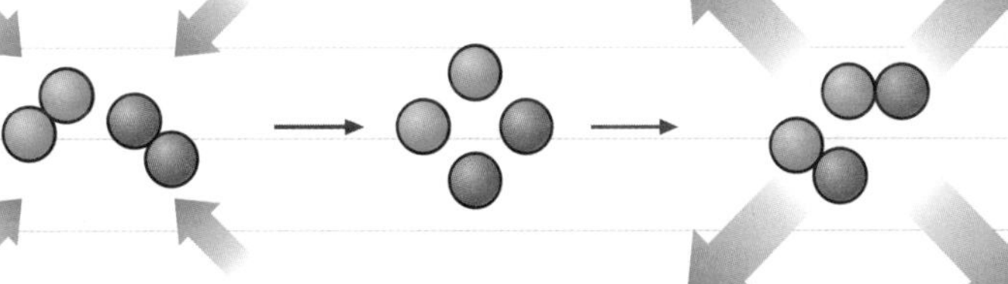

Endothermic reaction
The energy given out when the products form is *less than* the energy needed to break the bonds in the reactants. Overall, energy is taken in.

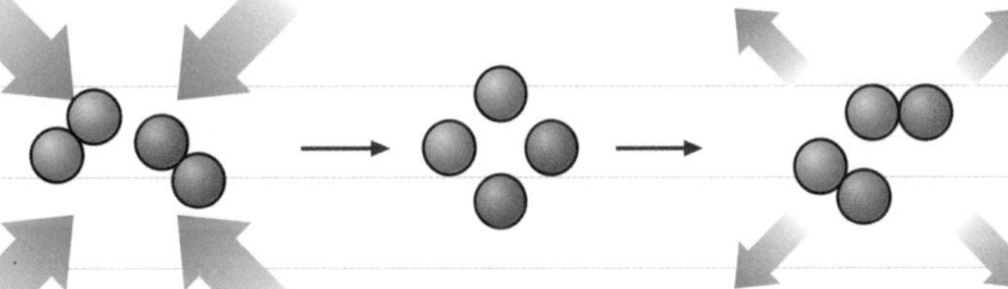

Now try this

Remember:
endothermic = energy in (energy enters)
exothermic = energy out (energy exits)

1. Methane burns in air to form carbon dioxide and water. Explain whether this is an exothermic or an endothermic reaction. **(2 marks)**
2. When baking powder is mixed with vinegar the temperature drops.
   (a) State whether this is an exothermic or endothermic reaction. **(1 mark)**
   (b) Explain which is the greatest: the energy taken in when the bonds in the reactants break, or the energy released when the bonds in the products form. **(2 marks)**

Rates of reaction 1

Reactions can happen at very different rates. It can take months for a piece of iron to go rusty, but it only takes a fraction of a second for a mixture of hydrogen and oxygen to explode.

Reactions happen when particles of different substances collide with each other. The more collisions there are every minute, the faster the rate of reaction.

A *faster* reaction is one that happens in a *shorter* time.

Changing the rate of a reaction

Temperature: reactions happen faster when the temperature is higher.

Concentration: reactions happen faster when more concentrated solutions are used.

Surface area: reactions happen faster when solid reactants are broken up into smaller pieces. Smaller pieces have bigger surface areas.

Catalyst: a catalyst speeds up a reaction without being used up itself.

The concentration of a solution is a measure of how much solute is dissolved in the solvent. A solution with a high concentration has a lot of particles in each cm^3.

Changing the *rate* of a reaction does not change the *amount* of the products formed, it just changes *how fast* they are formed.

Worked example

A student used this apparatus to investigate the factors that affect the rate of reaction. The magnesium ribbon reacts with the acid to produce hydrogen gas.

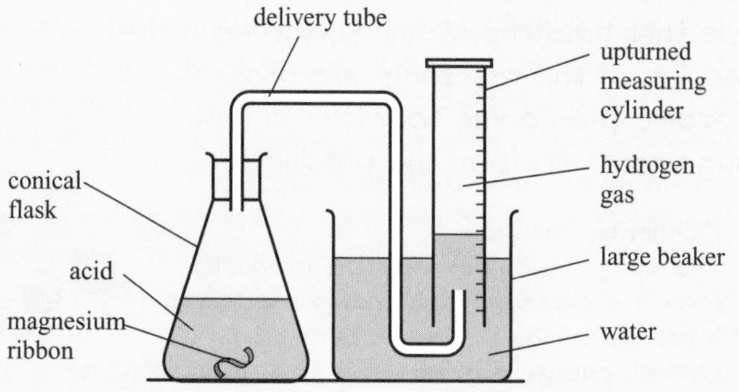

Explain how the student could use the apparatus shown above to investigate the effect of temperature on the rate of reaction.

They need to use the same amount of magnesium ribbon and the same concentration of acid each time. They should warm the acid to different temperatures.

They should fill the measuring cylinder with water, then add the magnesium to the acid and put the bung in the conical flask. They should measure how much hydrogen is in the measuring cylinder every minute for 5 minutes.

They should then repeat the experiment with the acid at different temperatures. They should plot all the results on the same graph to compare them. The graph with the steepest line will be the one with the fastest reaction.

EXAM ALERT!

You need to know the names of the pieces of apparatus you use in practical work. In a recent exam students were asked to label a diagram and more than four-fifths of them got no marks at all.

Students have struggled with exam questions similar to this - **be prepared!** ResultsPlus

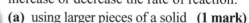

Now try this

target F-D

1. State whether each of these changes will increase or decrease the rate of reaction:

(a) using larger pieces of a solid **(1 mark)**

(b) a colder temperature **(1 mark)**

(c) more concentrated alkali. **(1 mark)**

Rates of reaction 2

Surface area

Reactions happen when the two reactants meet. If one of the reactants is a solid, breaking it up into smaller pieces provides a greater surface area. This makes the reaction happen faster.

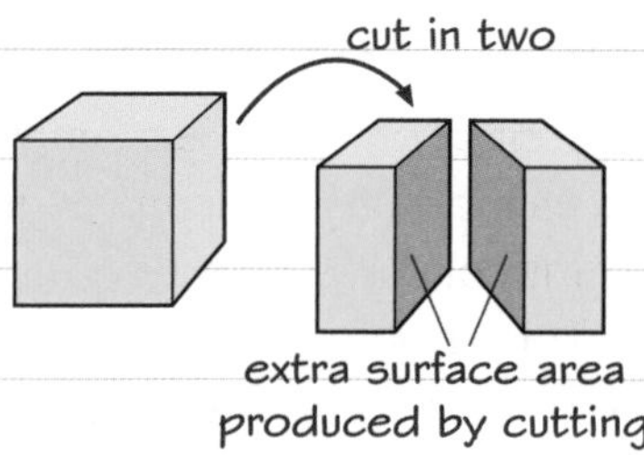

Catalysts

A catalyst is a substance that speeds up a reaction without being changed itself.

Worked example

Nickel is used as a catalyst in the manufacture of margarine. A manufacturer uses 1 kg of nickel to manufacture a batch of margarine. Explain how much nickel is left after the reaction.

1 kg is left. Catalysts do not get used up in reactions.

Catalytic converters

Catalytic converters are used in cars to reduce the pollution caused by waste gases from the engine.

Without catalytic converters

carbon monoxide
unburned fuel
carbon dioxide
water

With catalytic converters

carbon dioxide
water

unburned fuel / carbon monoxide + oxygen ⟶ carbon dioxide + water

The platinum catalyst in catalytic converters is made into a fine mesh to give it a large surface area. This allows more of the waste gases to come into contact with the catalyst and so helps to speed up the reaction.

Catalytic converters work best at high temperatures.

Now try this

1. A catalytic converter speeds up reactions in the exhaust gases from a car engine.
   - **(a)** Write down the reactants in these reactions. **(3 marks)**
   - **(b)** Write down the products of these reactions. **(2 marks)**

2. Explain why cars fitted with catalytic converters produce more carbon monoxide when they have just started their journey. **(3 marks)**

Relative masses

Relative atomic mass

The masses of atoms are so small that we do not talk about their mass in kilograms. Instead we use relative atomic mass (A_r). This is the mass of an atom compared with the mass of a carbon atom. Carbon has a relative atomic mass of 12. Magnesium atoms have twice as much mass as carbon atoms, so they have a relative atomic mass of 24.

Relative formula mass

The relative formula mass (M_r) is the sum of the relative atomic masses of all the atoms or ions in its formula.

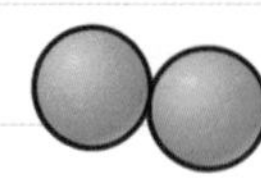

oxygen molecule – formula O_2
relative atomic mass of oxygen = 16
relative formula mass = 2 × 16
= 32

Some relative atomic masses are not whole numbers (such as chlorine, A_r = 35.5). This is because of different forms of the atom. You don't need to learn the reason for this in Additional Science.

Formulae

You have to understand what the numbers in chemical formulae mean before you can work out relative formula masses.

One molecule of water contains 2 atoms of hydrogen and 1 atom of oxygen.

H_2O

The 2 means that there are two atoms of the element *before* the number.

If there is no number, it means there is one atom of the element.

In aluminium nitrate, for each aluminium atom there are 3 nitrogen atoms and 9 oxygen atoms.

$Al(NO_3)_3$

This 3 only applies to the O, not to the N.

This 3 means there are three sets of the atoms inside the brackets.

Worked example

You do not need to learn any relative atomic masses.

Calculate the relative formula masses of

(a) carbon dioxide, CO_2 **(b)** zinc sulfate, $ZnSO_4$

Relative atomic masses: C = 12, O = 16, S = 32, Zn = 65

(a) CO_2 = 1 × C + 2 × O
M_r = (1 × 12) + (2 × 16)
= 44

(b) $ZnSO_4$ = 1 × Zn + 1 × S + 4 × O
M_r = 65 + 32 + (4 × 16)
= 161

EXAM ALERT!

Always show your working in a calculation. Even if you get the final answer wrong you may be able to show that you understand steps in the calculation.

Students have struggled with exam questions similar to this - **be prepared!** ResultsPlus

Now try this

1. Calculate the relative formula masses of the following compounds.
   (a) calcium oxide, (CaO) **(2 marks)**
   (b) ammonia, (NH_3) **(2 marks)**
   (c) calcium chloride, ($CaCl_2$). **(2 marks)**
   (Relative atomic masses: Ca = 40, Cl = 35.5, H = 1, N = 14, O = 16)

Empirical formulae

The empirical formula of a substance is the simplest whole number ratio of atoms or ions of each element in the substance. For example the empirical formula of sodium chloride is NaCl. This means that although sodium chloride forms a huge ionic structure with billions of ions, for every ion of sodium there is one chloride ion. For simple molecular compounds, the molecular formula is the actual number of atoms of each element in the molecule. For example, the molecular formula of water is H_2O.

The empirical formula is not always the same as the molecular formula. For example, ethene molecules (C_2H_4) each have two carbon atoms and four hydrogen atoms. Propene molecules (C_3H_6) each have three carbon atoms and six hydrogen atoms. The empirical formula for both of these compounds is CH_2.

Finding the empirical formula

Magnesium reacts with oxygen from the air to form magnesium oxide. You can find the empirical formula for magnesium oxide by heating magnesium in a crucible.

- Find the mass of the crucible before you start.
- Find the mass of some magnesium.
- Heat the magnesium in the crucible, lifting the lid occasionally to let some oxygen in.
- When all the magnesium has reacted, find the mass of the crucible and its contents.
- Subtract the mass of the empty crucible to find the mass of magnesium oxide formed.

Calculating empirical formulae

Worked example

A sample of magnesium chloride contains 5.0 g of magnesium and 14.8 g of chlorine. Calculate the empirical formula. (Relative atomic masses: Mg = 24, Cl = 35.5)

Mg: $\frac{5.0}{24} = 0.208$ Cl: $\frac{14.8}{35.5} = 0.417$

Divide each mass by the relative atomic mass of the element.

Mg: $\frac{0.208}{0.208} = 1$ Cl: $\frac{0.417}{0.208} = 2.005$ (round this to 2)

Empirical formula: $MgCl_2$

Divide *both* numbers by the smallest number to find the ratio. Round the answers if necessary.

EXAM ALERT!

Make sure you understand how to do these calculations. In a recent exam around two-thirds of pupils did not get full marks on a question like this.

Students have struggled with exam questions similar to this - **be prepared!** ResultsPlus

Now try this

1. A sample of sodium oxide contains 8 g of sodium and 2.78 g of oxygen. Calculate the empirical formula.
(Relative atomic masses: Na = 23, O = 16)
(3 marks)

Percentage composition

The percentage composition by mass of a compound is a way of working out how much of an element is present in a compound.

To work out the percentage by mass of an element in a compound you need to know:

- the number of atoms of the element in the compound
- the relative atomic mass (A_r) of the element
- the relative formula mass (M_r) of the compound (see page 62).

$$\text{percentage by mass of an element in a compound} = \text{number of atoms of element} \times \frac{A_r}{M_r} \times 100$$

Worked example

Calculate the percentage by mass of hydrogen in water (H_2O).

(Relative atomic masses: H = 1, O = 16)

There are 2 atoms of hydrogen in the formula.

A_r for hydrogen = 1

M_r for $H_2O = (2 \times 1) + (1 \times 16)$
$= 18$

Percentage of hydrogen by mass $= 2 \times \frac{1}{18} \times 100$
$= 11.1\%$

Worked example

Calculate the percentage by mass of oxygen in copper carbonate ($CuCO_3$).

(Relative atomic masses: Cu = 63.5, C = 12, O = 16)

You don't need to learn any relative atomic masses. The ones you need will always be given to you in an exam.

There are 3 atoms of oxygen in the formula.

A_r for oxygen = 16

M_r for $CuCO_3 = 63.5 + 12 + (3 \times 16)$
$= 123.5$

Percentage of oxygen by mass $= 3 \times \frac{16}{123.5} \times 100$
$= 38.9\%$

Check that your answer makes sense – the percentage you calculate should always be less than 100%.

Now try this

1. Calculate the percentage by mass of carbon in methane (CH_4). **(3 marks)**
(Relative atomic masses: C = 12, H = 1)

2. Calculate the percentage by mass of carbon in ethanol (C_2H_5OH). **(3 marks)**
(Relative atomic masses: C = 12, H = 1, O = 16)

Yields

The yield of a reaction is the amount of useful product you get at the end.

Actual and theoretical yields

You can calculate the mass of product you expect to get from a reaction using the balanced equation and the formula masses of the compounds. This is the theoretical yield of a reaction.

Don't worry! You don't need to be able to work out the theoretical yield.

Reactions do not always produce the amount of product predicted from the equation. The amount actually produced is called the actual yield.

Remember, the actual yield is sometimes the same as the theoretical yield, but usually it is less. The actual yield is never *more* than the theoretical yield.

The formula is

$$\text{percentage yield} = \frac{\text{actual yield}}{\text{theoretical yield}} \times 100\%$$

You may be given yields in kilograms instead of tonnes. It doesn't matter what the units are, as long as the units for the theoretical and actual yields are the same. Your answer will always be a percentage.

Worked example

Limestone is heated to produce calcium oxide.
The theoretical yield is 50 tonnes of calcium oxide.
The actual yield is 30 tonnes.
What is the percentage yield?

$$\text{percentage yield} = \frac{30 \text{ tonnes}}{50 \text{ tonnes}} \times 100\%$$

$$= 60\%$$

Why don't we always get full yield?

- A reaction does not always finish – there may be some reactants left at the end.
- Some of the reactants or products are lost during the process – such as liquids being spilled or left behind in a container.
- There may be unwanted reactions taking place – some reactants may react in a different way to make a different product.

Now try this

1. Explain the difference between theoretical yield and actual yield. **(2 marks)**
2. Iron is extracted from iron oxide. The theoretical yield of the reaction is 600 tonnes. The actual yield is 240 tonnes. Calculate the percentage yield. **(2 marks)**

Waste and profit

Most reactions have more than one product. Most reactions in the chemical industry produce substances other than the substance being manufactured. These are by-products. Some by-products can be sold, but some have no uses. These are waste products. The disposal of waste products can cause economic, environmental and social problems.

House prices could drop if there is a new chemical plant built, or if there are unpleasant smells.

Some waste products may accidentally escape and cause pollution.

People do not like living near landfill sites or incinerators. A new incinerator could cause house prices nearby to fall.

We are running out of landfill sites.

Many waste products that are not harmful still need to be disposed of. They may have to be transported to a landfill site or incinerator. Most commercial companies have to pay to use these facilities.

Some waste products are harmful, and treating them to make them safe costs money.

The smoke from incinerators is not as harmful as the substances that have been burned, but incinerating waste can still cause some air pollution.

Lorries taking waste to landfill sites or incinerators cause dust and disturbance.

Not all waste products are harmful. Some reactions produce water as a waste product, and this can be disposed of easily as long as it does not contain other substances.

Worked example

When iron is extracted from iron ore commercially, a waste product called slag is produced. Slag can be used to make cement. Explain how this helps the iron industry to make a profit.

The slag is useful, so the company can sell it to people who want to use it to make cement. If they can sell it, it also means that they do not have to pay to dump it in landfill sites. So they get extra money from selling the slag, and also do not have to pay to dispose of it, so they make more profit.

Now try this

1. (a) Describe two social problems that can be caused by disposing of waste products from the chemical industry. **(2 marks)**
   (b) Describe two economic problems. **(2 marks)**

Chemistry extended writing 4

Worked example

Modern cars have catalytic converters to reduce the amount of air pollution caused by their exhaust fumes. Explain how catalytic converters reduce air pollution. Your answers should include how they change the exhaust gases, and why they need to be hot to work properly. **(6 marks)**

Sample answer 1

The catalytic converter speeds up reactions in the exhaust to remove all the polluting gases. It does this best when it is hot, so it needs to be hot to work properly. All cars in the UK have to have these.

This is a basic answer. It correctly states that the catalytic converter speeds up reactions, but it is not true that this removes all polluting gases (carbon dioxide is still a pollutant). It does not *explain* why the catalytic converter needs to be hot to work well.

The last sentence is correct, but the question did not ask for this kind of information so there will be no marks for saying this.

Sample answer 2

The exhaust gases from car engines include carbon dioxide, carbon monoxide, water and some petrol (hydrocarbon) that hasn't burned properly. The catalytic converter changes the carbon monoxide and petrol to carbon dioxide and water. It does this by having a catalyst that speeds up the reaction. It needs to be hot because reactions happen faster when they are hot. Carbon dioxide is a polluting gas because it causes global warming, but it is not as bad as having the carbon monoxide and petrol in the air because carbon monoxide is toxic.

This is a very good answer. It contains all the details needed, and is written using correct spelling and grammar. It also contains scientific words such as 'catalyst' and 'hydrocarbon'. You are not *expected* to include facts such as carbon monoxide being toxic, as that was part of the Science course, but you get credit in these long questions for including any correct facts, as long as they are *relevant* to the question.

Now try this

1. The apparatus in the diagram can be used to investigate rates of reaction. When magnesium reacts with hydrochloric acid, the reaction produces hydrogen gas. The gas escapes from the mixture, and so the mixture gets lighter. You can investigate how fast the reaction happens by seeing how fast the mass changes. Explain how you can use this apparatus to show how the rate of reaction changes when the concentration of acid changes. Your answer should include the result you would expect to get. **(6 marks)**

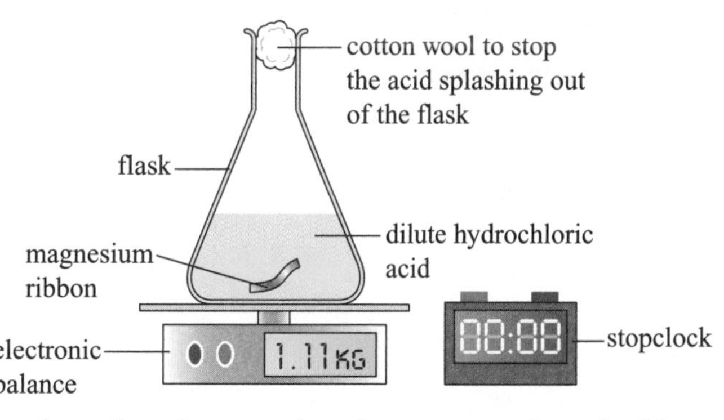

Chemistry extended writing 5

Worked example

Magnesium reacts with hydrochloric acid to form hydrogen and magnesium chloride. Zinc also reacts with hydrochloric acid, and produces hydrogen and zinc chloride solution.

Describe how you could carry out an investigation to find out which of these reactions is the most exothermic. **(6 marks)**

Sample answer 1

I will put some magnesium into acid and measure the temperature before the reaction and after the reaction has finished. I will do the same thing with the zinc.

This is a basic answer. The outline of the investigation is correct, but the answer also needs to describe how to make the investigation a fair test, and how the student will decide which reaction is the most exothermic.

Sample answer 2

An exothermic reaction releases heat energy, so the temperature of the mixture will go up. You can measure how exothermic a reaction is by measuring the temperature before and after the reaction. Do this in an insulated cup to make sure not too much heat escapes.

Put the magnesium into acid and measure the temperature at the beginning and the end. Do the same with the zinc. To make this a fair test and allow the results to be compared, use the same mass of metal each time, the same volume of acid and the same concentration.

You can get more reliable results by doing each experiment several times, and taking an average of the result. You should wear safety glasses because acids can damage your eyes.

This is an excellent, detailed answer. It explains how to carry out the investigation, including how to make it a fair test and how to stay safe.

Now try this

1. Explain what the 'yield' of a reaction is, and why the actual yield is usually less than the theoretical yield. **(6 marks)**

Static electricity

Atoms

Atoms have a nucleus containing protons and neutrons. Electrons move around the nucleus of an atom. An atom has the same number of protons and electrons, so the + and – charges balance and the atom has no overall charge.

Electrostatic charges

Insulating materials can be given an electrostatic charge by rubbing two materials together. Electrons are transferred from one material to the other. The material that has gained electrons has a negative charge. The material that has lost electrons has a positive charge equal in size to the negative charge.

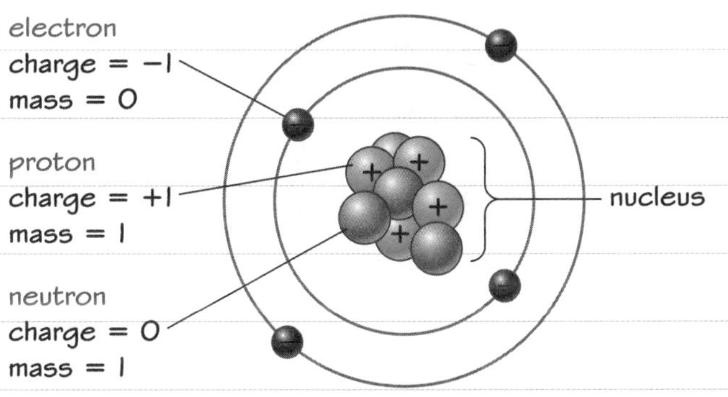
electron
charge = −1
mass = 0
proton
charge = +1
mass = 1
neutron
charge = 0
mass = 1
nucleus

EXAM ALERT!

In a recent exam question on static electricity about half of students did not achieve any marks. Remember it is always the **electrons** that move. If a material has a positive charge it is because it has *lost* some electrons and so now it has more protons than electrons.

Students have struggled with this topic in recent exams - **be prepared!** ResultsPlus

Charging by induction

A charged object (such as a plastic comb) can attract uncharged objects (such as small pieces of paper). This happens because the comb induces a charge in the pieces of paper.

balloon
wall
The balloon has a negative charge.

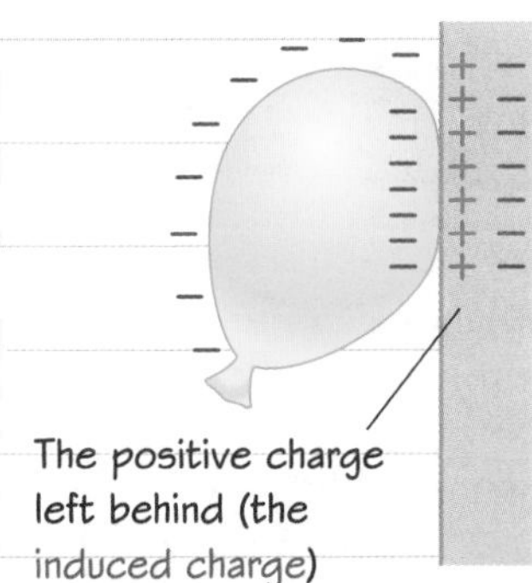
The electrons in the wall are repelled and move away.
The positive charge left behind (the induced charge) attracts the negative charge on the balloon.

Now try this

target G-D

1. Name the particles in an atom that:
   (a) have a relative mass of 1 **(1 mark)**
   (b) are in the nucleus **(1 mark)**
   (c) have a negative charge. **(1 mark)**

target D-C

2. You rub a comb with a cloth. The comb gets a positive charge.
   (a) Explain how particles have been transferred to give the comb a positive charge. **(4 marks)**
   (b) Explain what will happen if you hold the comb close to a positively charged rod hanging on a thread. **(2 marks)**

Uses and dangers

Shocks and earthing

You can sometimes build up a charge of static electricity as you move around. If you then touch a door or other object you may feel a shock. This happens as electrons move to 'cancel out' the charge on you. This is called earthing.

Lightning happens when a charge of static electricity builds up in clouds. When the charge is big enough, charged particles can flow through the air. The energy released by this causes light and sound. Lightning can kill living things and damage buildings.

Remember that it is always the *electrons* that move. If you have a positive charge, electrons will move from earth onto you. If you have a negative charge, electrons will move from you to earth.

If you have a negative charge...

...electrons will flow from you to earth.

Using static electricity

Static electricity is useful in paint spraying and insecticide sprayers.

Nozzle of paint sprayer connected to electricity supply. → Droplets all get the **same kind** of static charge so they spread out evenly. → The object being painted is given the **opposite** charge to the paint. → The paint is attracted to the object being painted and less paint is wasted.

Worked example

Explain how static electricity can be dangerous when aeroplanes are refuelling, and how this problem is solved.

Static electricity can build up on an aeroplane as it flies. When it is being refuelled, the static charge may cause a spark when the nozzle of a fuel tanker touches the aeroplane. This could cause an explosion if it ignites fuel vapour.

A conducting wire called a bonding line is used to earth any static charge on the aeroplane before refuelling starts. Electrons can flow along the wire to earth to neutralise the static charge on the aeroplane.

A similar problem can occur when tankers deliver fuel to filling stations. To stop explosions the hose used to fill the tanks is made of a conducting material. Any charge can be earthed without causing sparks.

Now try this

1. You walk across a carpet and then touch a metal door knob. Explain why you may get a shock. **(2 marks)**
2. Describe one way in which static electricity can be dangerous. **(1 mark)**
3. Explain how static electricity is used in paint spraying. **(4 marks)**

Electric currents

Direct current

An electric current in a wire is a flow of electrons. The current supplied by cells and batteries is direct current (d.c.). In a direct current the electrons all flow in the same direction.

cell

Electrons are pushed out of one end of the cell.

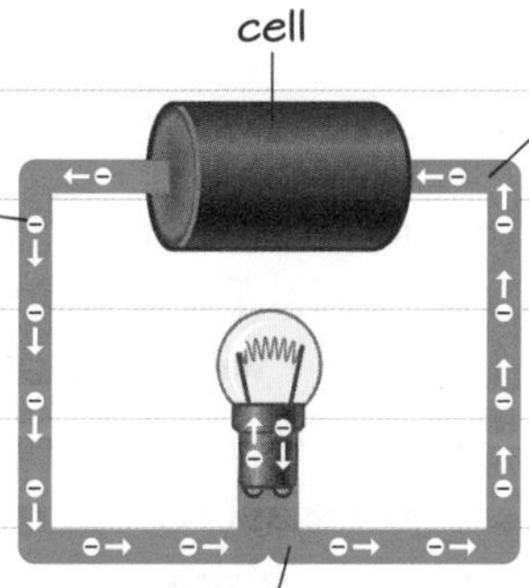

Electrons flow round to the other end of the cell.

There must be a complete circuit for the electrons to flow.

Charge and current

The size of a current is a measure of how much charge flows past a point each second. It is the rate of flow of charged particles. The unit of charge is the coulomb (C). 1 ampere (amp) is one coulomb of charge per second.

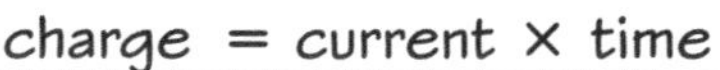

charge = current × time

$Q = I \times t$ Q = charge (coulombs, C)
I = current (amp, A)
t = time (seconds, s)

Don't get the units and quantities confused. The *units* have sensible abbreviations (C for coulombs, A for amps). The symbols for the quantities are not as easy to remember (Q stands for charge, and I for current). The exam paper will give you the equations in words as well as symbols, so don't worry too much if you cannot remember what Q and I stand for.

Worked example

There is a 10 A current in a circuit. Calculate the amount of charge that flows through the circuit in 2 minutes.

You need to remember the correct units for each quantity. The equations will be given to you in the exam, but not the units!

Time must be in seconds:

2 minutes = 2 × 60 seconds
= 120 seconds

$Q = I \times t$
= 10 A × 120 s
= 1200 C

EXAM ALERT!

Always show your working in a calculation. Even if you get the final answer wrong you may be able to show that you understand steps in the calculation.

Students have struggled with exam questions similar to this - **be prepared!** ResultsPlus

Now try this

target G-F

1. Name the charged particles that flow when there is an electric current in a wire. **(1 mark)**

target G-E

2. Describe how charged particles move in a direct current. **(1 mark)**

target G-D

3. A 5 A current flows for 20 seconds. Calculate the amount of charge that has passed through the circuit. **(3 marks)**

Current and voltage

Measuring current and voltage

The current in an electric circuit is measured using an ammeter. The ammeter is placed in a circuit in series with the other components.

The potential difference (voltage) across a component is measured using a voltmeter. The voltmeter is placed in parallel with the component.

Potential difference is another name for voltage, so you can use either term.

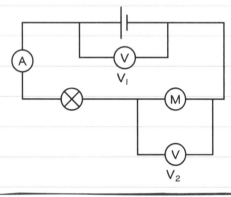

You need to learn the symbols for the different circuit components shown here.

Voltmeter V_1 is measuring the potential difference across the cell. Voltmeter V_2 is measuring the potential difference across the motor.

Worked example

How does the size of the current change if the potential difference (voltage) of the power supply is changed?

If the potential difference is increased, the current increases. If the potential difference is made smaller, the current gets smaller.

Current in parallel circuits

The current in a series circuit is the same everywhere. A parallel circuit has more than one path for the current to flow through. The current splits up when it reaches a junction and comes back together when the wires rejoin.

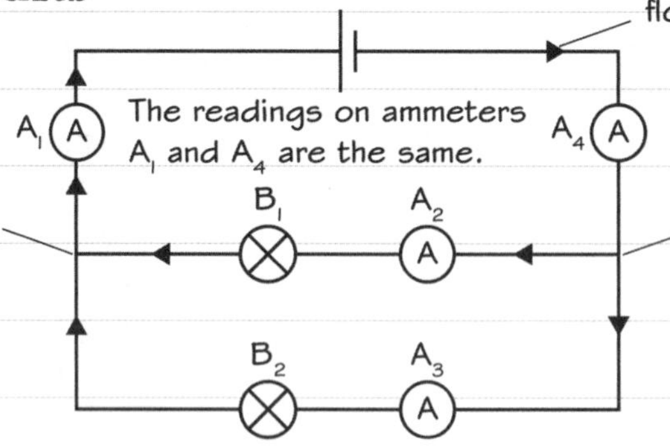

flow of electrons

The electrons join up again here.

The number of electrons leaving this junction each second is the same as the total number arriving each second.

The readings on ammeters A_2 and A_3 add up to the reading shown on A_1 and A_4.

Now try this

1. Name the instrument used to measure current. **(1 mark)**
2. **(a)** Draw a series circuit with one cell, one motor and one bulb. **(4 marks)**
   (b) Add an ammeter to your circuit. **(1 mark)**
   (c) Add a voltmeter to your circuit to measure the potential difference across the bulb. **(1 mark)**

Resistance, current and voltage

Resistance

The resistance of a component is a way of measuring how hard it is for electricity to flow through it. The units for resistance are ohms (Ω).

The resistance of a whole circuit depends on the resistances of the different components in the circuit. The higher the total resistance, the smaller the current.

resistance UP, current goes DOWN

The resistance of a circuit can be changed by putting different resistors into the circuit, or by using a variable resistor. The resistance of a variable resistor can be changed using a slider or knob.

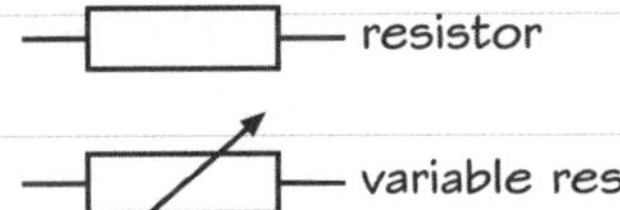

Circuit calculations

You can calculate the resistance of a component by measuring the current and voltage and then rearranging this formula:

potential difference = current × resistance

$V = I \times R$ V = voltage (or potential difference) (volts, V)
I = current (amps, A)
R = resistance (ohms, Ω)

Worked example

Resistor A has a current of 3 A flowing through it when the voltage across it is 15 V.
What is its resistance? Use $R = \frac{V}{I}$

$$R = \frac{15\text{ V}}{3\text{ A}} = 5\ \Omega$$

You don't need to remember this formula, as it will be given to you in the exam. You *do* need to be able to use it, and to remember the correct units for the different quantities.

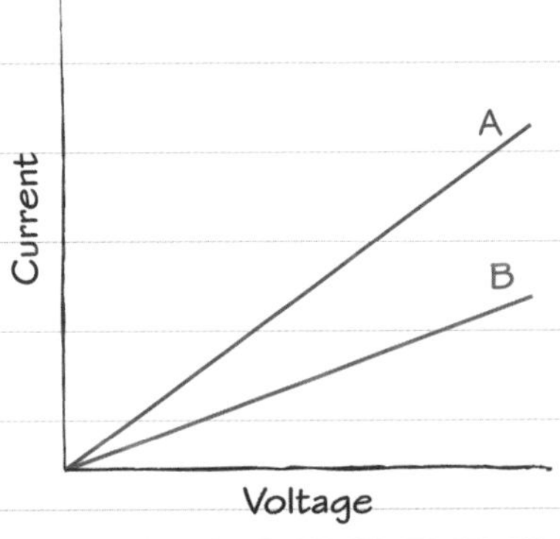

The steeper line shows that resistor A has a lower resistance than resistor B.

A graph of current against voltage for a resistor is a straight line if the temperature of the resistor does not change.

In the example above, resistor A had a current of 3 A when the voltage was 15 V. Resistor B has a higher resistance than Resistor A so the current will be lower for the same voltage.

Now try this

1. A circuit has a resistance of 10 Ω and a cell with a potential difference of 3 V. State what will happen to the current if:
   (a) the cell is exchanged for one with a potential difference of 6 V **(1 mark)**
   (b) the resistance is decreased to 8 Ω. **(1 mark)**

target E-D

2. Calculate the voltage needed to make a 2 A current flow through a 15 Ω resistor. **(3 marks)**
3. A 6 V battery provides a current of 2 A in a circuit. Calculate the resistance of the circuit. Use $R = \frac{V}{I}$. **(3 marks)**

Changing resistances

Some electrical components change their resistance depending on the potential difference or the conditions surrounding them.

Filament lamps

Filament lamps get hotter as the voltage across them increases. This increases their resistance. The higher the temperature, the higher the resistance.

voltage UP, resistance UP

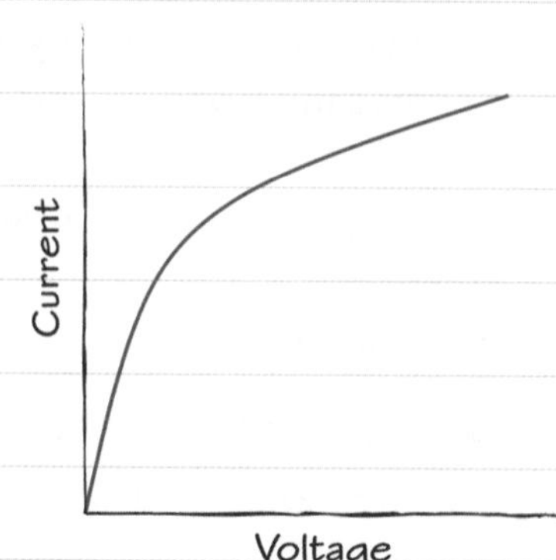

The line gets shallower at higher voltages, showing that the resistance is increasing.

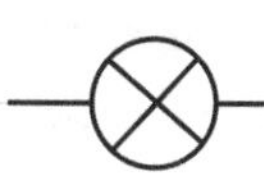

Diodes

When the current flows in one direction diodes behave like fixed resistors. The resistance does not change if the voltage changes. Diodes only conduct electricity in one direction. They do not allow current to flow in the other direction.

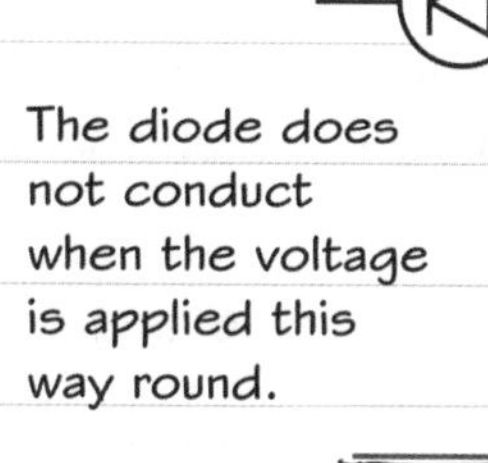

The diode does not conduct when the voltage is applied this way round.

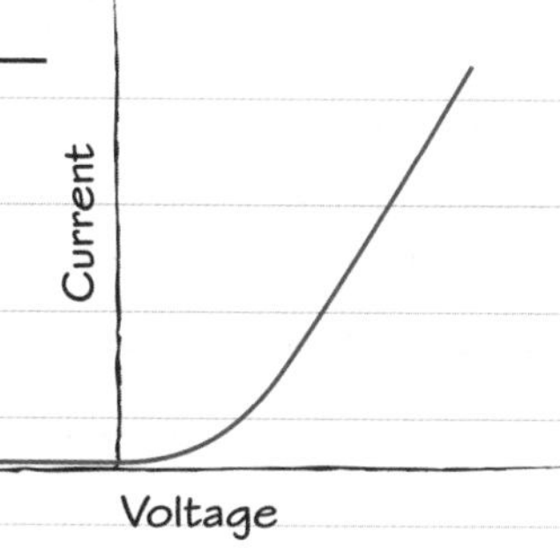

Light-dependent resistors

The resistance of a light-dependent resistor (LDR) is large in the dark. The resistance gets less if light shines on it. The brighter the light, the lower the resistance.

brightness UP, resistance DOWN

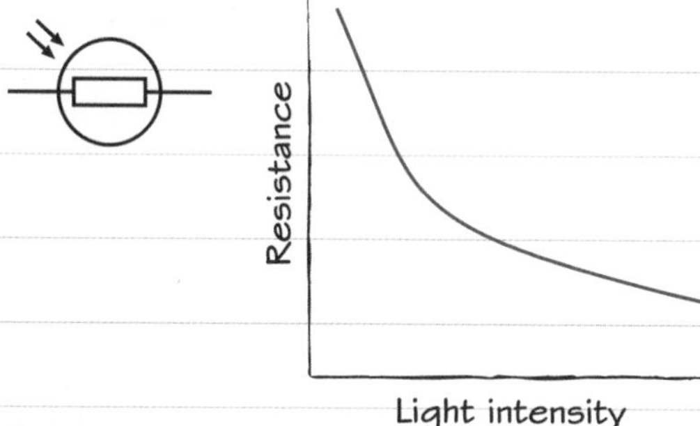

Thermistors

The resistance of a thermistor depends on its temperature. The higher the temperature, the lower the resistance.

temperature UP, resistance DOWN

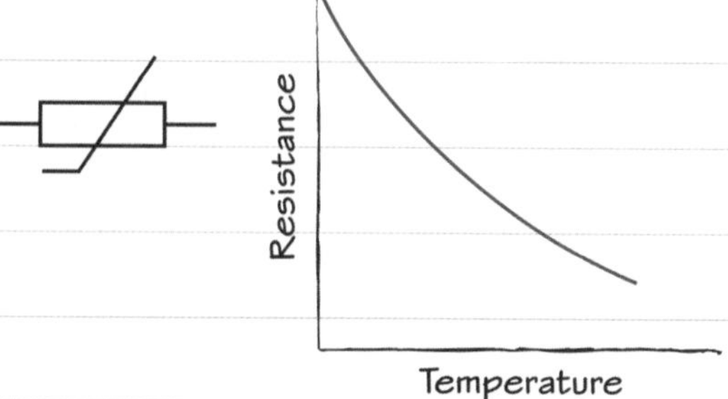

Now try this

1. Name a component that only allows electricity to flow in one direction. **(1 mark)**
2. Name a component that changes its resistance when its temperature changes. **(1 mark)**
3. Explain how the resistance of a filament lamp changes when the potential difference across it increases. **(2 marks)**

Transferring energy

Energy is transferred to a resistor when a current flows through it. This energy transfer heats the resistor. The heating effect is useful in electric fires or electric cookers. Some heating is not useful, such as when energy is wasted as heat energy in motors or other electric components.

Power

The power of an appliance is the energy transferred per second. The unit for power is the watt (W).
1 watt = 1 joule per second.

Don't get watts and joules mixed up. Remember: joules are for energy, watts are for power (energy per second).

electrical power (watt, W) = current (amp, A) × potential difference (volt, V)

$$P = I \times V$$

Energy

The total energy transferred by an appliance depends on its power and how long it is switched on.

energy transferred (joule, J) = current (amp, A) × potential difference (volt, V) × time (second, s)

$$E = I \times V \times t$$

Worked example

A travel kettle uses electricity from a 12 V car battery. The current is 15 A.
Calculate the energy it transfers in one minute.

1 minute = 60 seconds
energy = 15 A × 12 V × 60 s
= 10 800 J

Be careful with your units. If you are given a time in minutes, you must convert it to seconds by multiplying by 60.

Now try this

1. State the units for
   (a) power **(1 mark)**
   (b) energy. **(1 mark)**
2. A motor is connected to a 6 V cell. The current is 0.5 A.
   Calculate the power of the motor. **(3 marks)**
3. A heater uses the mains supply of 230 V. The current through it is 9 A.
   Calculate the energy it transfers in 10 minutes. **(4 marks)**

Physics extended writing 1

When answering extended writing questions you should try to:

- ✓ Apply your scientific knowledge.
- ✓ Present your answer in a logical and organised way.
- ✓ Write a full answer and make sure that your spelling, punctuation and grammar are as good as you can make them.

Worked example

The resistance of a thermistor decreases as its temperature increases. The resistance at a particular temperature will be different for different thermistors.

You are given two different thermistors. Explain how you would produce a graph of resistance against temperature for each thermistor. **(6 marks)**

Sample answer 1

I will measure the resistance of each thermistor at different temperatures and then plot a graph of my results.

This answer would probably not gain any marks. It is not incorrect, but you need to provide much more detail than this about how you would carry out the tests.

Sample answer 2

I will put a thermistor into a circuit with an ammeter and a voltmeter and a cell, and write down the readings. I will then dip the thermistor into warm water and take the readings again. I will repeat this with warmer and warmer water, until I have got readings for about 5 or 6 different temperatures. I will work out the resistance from the current and voltage readings, and plot a graph.

I will keep safe by not spilling water onto any of the rest of the circuit, and using a low voltage cell.

This is a basic answer. It describes the measurements that need to be taken to work out the resistance of the thermistor at different temperatures and how the temperature of the thermistor will be changed. It also describes some safety precautions.

This answer would be improved by explaining how the temperature of the water is to be measured, how the water will be heated, and suggesting which temperatures to use.

Now try this

1. A polythene rod is given a negative charge of static electricity by rubbing it with a cloth. An acetate rod gets a positive charge when it is rubbed. The charged rods can be used to pick up small pieces of paper.

Explain what happens during the rubbing to charge these rods, and why a charged rod can pick up pieces of paper. **(6 marks)**

You can break this answer up into three parts: what happens when the polythene rod is rubbed, what happens when the acetate rod is rubbed, and what happens in the pieces of paper when a charged rod is brought close to them. You only need to describe how one of the rods picks up paper.

Vectors and velocity

Vectors

Some quantities are vectors. They have a direction as well as a size. Vectors include:

- displacement
- force
- velocity
- acceleration.

Calculating speed

Speed is calculated from a distance and a time.

$$\text{speed (m/s)} = \frac{\text{distance (m)}}{\text{time (s)}}$$

Distance–time graphs

Al is riding his bike. The distance–time graph tells us about his journey.

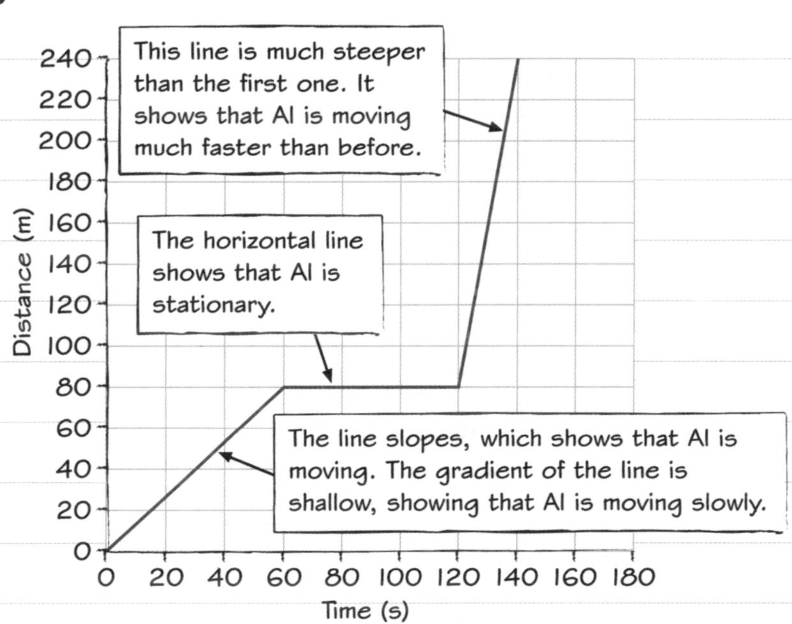
This line is much steeper than the first one. It shows that Al is moving much faster than before.
The horizontal line shows that Al is stationary.
The line slopes, which shows that Al is moving. The gradient of the line is shallow, showing that Al is moving slowly.
Distance (m)
0
20
40
60
80
100
120
140
160
180
200
220
240
Time (s)
0 20 40 60 80 100 120 140 160 180

Worked example

Calculate Al's speed during the last part of his journey, using the gradient of the line on the graph.

Distance = 240 m − 80 m = 160 m

Time = 140 s − 120 s = 20 s

Speed = $\frac{160\text{ m}}{20\text{ s}}$

= 8 m/s

Find the change in distance from the graph, and the change in time.

Use these numbers in the equation for speed.

Now try this

target
G-D

1. Explain the difference between a distance and a displacement. **(2 marks)**

target
D-C

2. Calculate Al's speed for the first part of his journey. **(4 marks)**

Velocity and acceleration

Acceleration

Acceleration is a change in velocity.
Acceleration is a vector quantity.

$$\text{Acceleration (m/s}^2) = \frac{\text{change in velocity (m/s)}}{\text{time taken (s)}}$$

$$a = \frac{(v - u)}{t}$$

a is the acceleration
v is the final velocity
u is the initial velocity
t is the time taken

Worked example

A car travelling at 20 m/s slows down to 10 m/s in 4 seconds.
Calculate its acceleration.

$$\text{acceleration} = \frac{(10\text{ m/s} - 20\text{ m/s})}{4\text{ s}} = \frac{-10\text{ m/s}}{4\text{ s}} = -2.5\text{ m/s}^2$$

Slowing down is also an 'acceleration'. An object slowing down will have a negative acceleration. If you remember to always put the final velocity first in the equation, your answer will have the correct sign.

Velocity–time graphs

This velocity–time graph shows how the velocity of a train along a straight track changes with time.

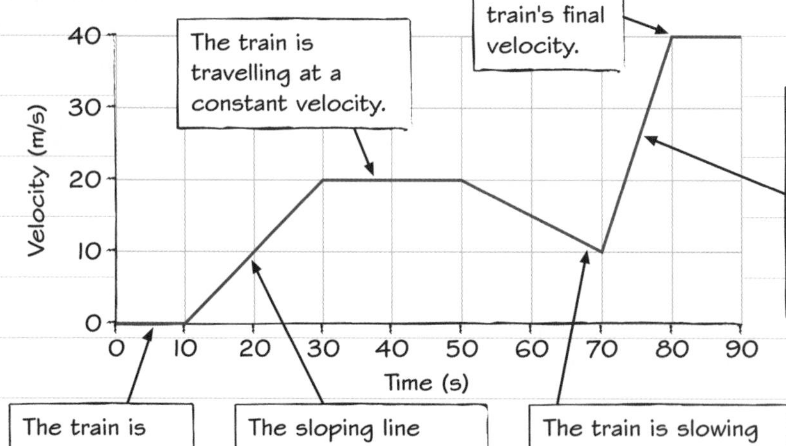

Velocity (m/s)
0
10
20
30
40
Time (s)
0
10
20
30
40
50
60
70
80
90
The train is travelling at a constant velocity.
This is the train's final velocity.
The train is accelerating. The line is steeper so its acceleration is greater than it was between 10 and 30 seconds.
The train is stationary (its velocity is 0).
The sloping line shows that the train is accelerating.
The train is slowing down (its velocity is getting less).

Watch out! Check which kind of graph you are looking at. The slope of the line means different things on the different types of graph.

	Distance–time graph	Velocity–time graph
horizontal line	stationary	constant velocity
sloping line	constant speed	accelerating

Now try this

target F-D

1. Look at the velocity–time graph. Describe the train's journey in words. **(3 marks)**

2. Calculate the acceleration of the train between 10 seconds and 30 seconds. **(3 marks)**

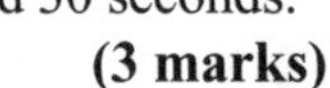

target D-C

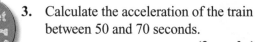

3. Calculate the acceleration of the train between 50 and 70 seconds. **(3 marks)**

Resultant forces

If there is more than one force on a body, all the forces can be combined into a resultant force.

Free-body diagrams

A force is a vector quantity, because it has a direction as well as a size. A free-body force diagram represents all the forces on a single body. Larger forces are shown using longer arrows.

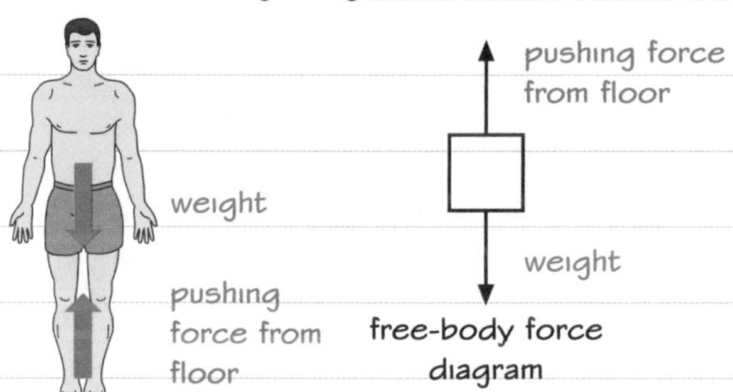

Action and reaction forces

Two touching objects exert forces on each other.

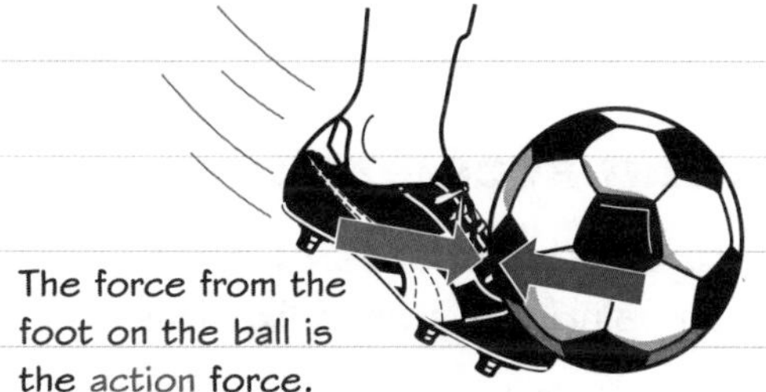

The force from the foot on the ball is the action force.
The ball exerts an equal and opposite reaction force on the boot.

Watch out! Free-body diagrams are for forces on the same body. Action and reaction forces are forces on separate bodies.

Worked example

Explain the effect that each of these forces will have on a car.

(a) 300 N forward force from the engine, 200 N drag.

(a) Resultant force = 300 N − 200 N = 100 N. The car will accelerate in the direction of the resultant force. Its velocity will increase.

A resultant force acting in the opposite direction to the movement of a body will slow it down.

(b) 200 N forward force from the engine, 400 N friction from brakes.

(b) Resultant = 200 N − 400 N = −200 N (200 N acting backwards). The car will accelerate in the direction of the resultant force. This is in the opposite direction to its velocity, so the car will slow down.

(c) 300 N forward force, 300 N drag.

(c) Resultant = 0 N, so the car will continue to move at the same velocity.

Now try this

1. There is a 100 N forwards force on a car, and a 30 N backwards force.
(a) Calculate the resultant force. **(2 marks)**
(b) Explain what will happen to the car. **(2 marks)**

2. A girl is sitting on a chair.
(a) Draw a free-body diagram to represent the forces on her. **(2 marks)**
(b) Describe an action–reaction pair of forces for the girl and the chair. **(2 marks)**

Forces and acceleration

Force and mass

The acceleration produced by a resultant force depends on the size of the force and the mass of the object.

- The greater the force, the greater the acceleration for a constant mass.
- The greater the mass, the smaller the acceleration for a constant force.

Investigating acceleration

You can investigate the effects of mass on acceleration using apparatus like this.

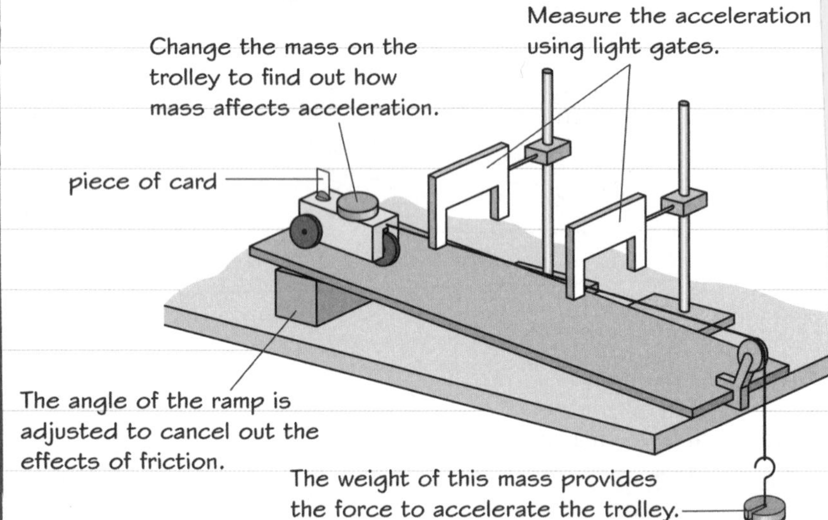

Measure the acceleration using light gates.
Change the mass on the trolley to find out how mass affects acceleration.
piece of card
The angle of the ramp is adjusted to cancel out the effects of friction.
The weight of this mass provides the force to accelerate the trolley.

You can also use this apparatus to investigate the effect of force on acceleration. You can increase the force by increasing the number of masses on the end of the string. The masses on the pulley are accelerating as well as the trolley, and you need to keep the total mass constant to make sure the test is fair. The best way to do this is to start with several masses on the trolley, and transfer these to the pulley one by one to increase the force.

EXAM ALERT!

Only about one in ten students gained any marks on a similar question recently. Remember that there will also be forces of friction and air resistance acting, so in real life a car engine would need to produce a larger force than this to achieve 2.5 m/s^2 acceleration.

Students have struggled with exam questions similar to this - **be prepared!**

Worked example

A car has a mass of 1200 kg. It accelerates at 2.5 m/s^2. Calculate the force provided by its engine using the formula:

force (N) = mass (kg) × acceleration (m/s^2)

$F = m \times a$

$F = 1200\text{ kg} \times 2.5\text{ m/s}^2$

$= 3000\text{ N}$

Now try this

1. Explain why it is easier to get an empty shopping trolley moving than a full one. **(2 marks)**

2. A 30 kg greyhound accelerates at 5 m/s^2. Calculate the force it produces. **(2 marks)**
3. A 1200 kg family car decelerates at 4 m/s^2. Calculate the force provided by its brakes. **(2 marks)**

Terminal velocity

Mass and weight

Mass:
- is the amount of matter in an object
- is measured in kilograms (kg).

Weight:
- is the force of gravity on an object
- is measured in newtons (N).

On Earth, every kilogram of mass is pulled down with a force of 10 N.

weight (N) = mass (kg) × gravitational field strength (N/kg)

$$W = m \times g$$

The mass must always be in kilograms.

Falling

The force of gravity on a large mass is greater than on a small mass, but the large mass also needs a greater force to accelerate it. The two effects cancel out, and so all masses fall at the same rate in a vacuum. This acceleration due to gravity is 10 m/s^2 on the Earth.

EXAM ALERT!

Just over one in ten students achieved full marks on a recent exam question on this subject.

On Earth, air resistance affects the acceleration of the object, so things do not all fall at the same rate. If you are asked to describe the forces on a falling body in an exam question, don't forget the air resistance!

Students have struggled with this topic in recent exams - **be prepared!** ResultsPlus

Terminal velocity

Just after jumping:
velocity = very small
air resistance = very small
resultant force = weight
acceleration = 10 m/s^2

5 seconds later:
velocity greater
air resistance = about half of weight
resultant force = weight − air resistance
acceleration is decreasing

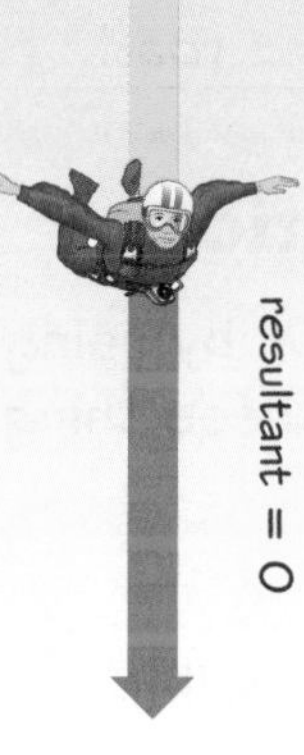

About 12 seconds after jumping:
velocity maximum
= terminal velocity
air resistance = weight
resultant force = 0 N
acceleration = 0 m/s^2

Now try this

1. Calculate the weight of a 62 kg woman. **(2 marks)**
2. Calculate the weight of a 35 g mouse. **(3 marks)**
3. A skydiver has a weight of 700 N. She has reached terminal velocity. Explain the size of her:
   (a) acceleration **(2 marks)**
   (b) air resistance. **(2 marks)**

Stopping distances

It takes time for a moving car to come to a stop, and the car is still moving during this time. Understanding the factors that affect stopping distances is important for road safety.

danger appears

driver brakes

car stopped

thinking distance = the distance the car travels while the driver reacts to the danger and applies the brakes

braking distance = the distance the car travels while it is slowing down

stopping distance = thinking distance + braking distance

Factors affecting stopping distance

It takes more force to stop a vehicle with more mass – so if two vehicles with the same brakes try to stop at the same time the one with the greater mass will travel further while it is braking.

Factor	Thinking distance	Braking distance
Mass of vehicle	no change	*increases*
Speed	*increases*	*increases*
Reaction time	*increases* (if reaction time is slow)	no change
State of brakes	no change	*increases* if brakes not working properly
State of road	no change	*increases* if road surface slippery
Amount of friction between tyres and road	no change	*increases* if friction is less

Reaction time is increased if the driver is tired, or has been drinking alcohol or taking drugs.

Remember that factors such as mass, brakes and road surface only affect the braking distance, not the thinking distance.

Investigating friction

You can investigate friction by using a forcemeter to pull blocks along different surfaces. You would need to keep these things the same:

- the size of the block
- the mass of the block
- the speed at which you pull it.

Now try this

target G-E

1. Name one factor that:
   (a) only affects the thinking distance **(1 mark)**
   (b) only affects the braking distance **(1 mark)**
   (c) affects both the thinking distance and the braking distance. **(1 mark)**

target G-D

2. Explain why the stopping distance is longer if a driver is tired. **(2 marks)**

Momentum

The momentum of a moving object depends on its mass and its velocity. Momentum is a vector quantity.

momentum = mass × velocity
(kg m/s) (kg) (m/s)

Momentum is mass multiplied by velocity, so the units for momentum are a combination of the units for mass and velocity.

Collisions

When two objects collide, the total momentum before the collision is the same as the total momentum after the collision, providing no external forces act. Momentum is conserved.

Before collision...

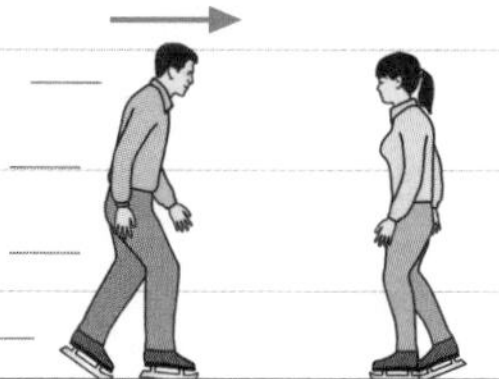

m = 50 kg v = 5 m/s	m = 50 kg v = 0 m/s

Total momentum
= 50 kg × 5 m/s + 50 kg × 0 m/s
= 250 kg m/s

After collision...

m = 100 kg v = 2.5 m/s

Total momentum
= 100 kg × 2.5 m/s
= 250 kg m/s

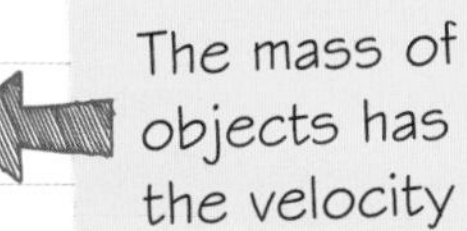

The mass of the moving objects has doubled, so the velocity has halved.

Worked example

An ice skater has a mass of 65 kg. She is moving at 10 m/s when she collides with a stationary spectator standing on the ice and holds onto him. The spectator has a mass of 80 kg. Calculate the velocity of the skater and spectator together.
Use velocity = momentum/mass.

momentum = 65 kg × 10 m/s = 650 kg m/s

total mass = 65 kg + 80 kg
= 145 kg

velocity = $\frac{650 \text{ kg m/s}}{145 \text{ kg}}$
= 4.48 m/s

Remember that the total momentum is the same before and after the collision.

Check your answer. The mass has gone up so the velocity must be less than the original value.

Now try this

1. A motorcycle and a car are both moving at 20 m/s. Explain which one has the largest momentum. **(2 marks)**
2. A car has a mass of 1200 kg. It is moving at 15 m/s. Calculate its momentum. **(3 marks)**
3. A moving van crashes into the back of a stationary car and the two vehicles move along the road together. Explain why the velocity of the two vehicles is less than the original velocity of the van. **(3 marks)**

Momentum and safety

Changing momentum

Momentum is conserved in collisions if there are no other forces involved. The momentum of a moving object can change if a force is applied. A larger force produces a greater rate of change of momentum (the momentum changes faster).

Car safety features

crumple zones squash and reduce the momentum gradually.

airbags help to slow you down gradually.

seat belts stretch to slow you down gradually.

Bubble wrap is used to protect fragile items. If something hits the wrapped object the air in the bubbles squashes and reduces the force on the object.

Worked example

Use the idea of rate of change of momentum to explain how seat belts work.

Seat belts stretch and slow you down gradually, instead of you coming to a stop suddenly when you hit the dashboard. When you slow down more gradually the rate of change of momentum is less and so there are smaller forces on you. You will be less likely to be injured in a crash.

Investigating crumple zones

You can use apparatus like this to investigate the effectiveness of crumple zones. Greater impact forces will cause bigger dents in the Plasticine®.

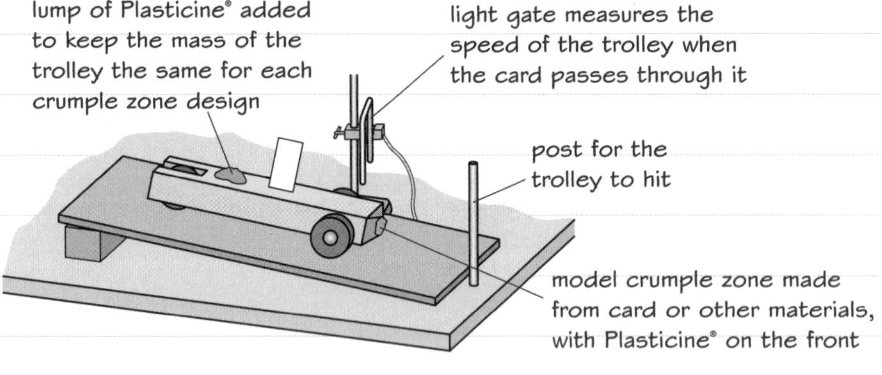

You need to keep these things the same for each crumple zone design to allow you to compare your results:

- speed of trolley
- mass of trolley
- size and shape of the object that it hits.

Now try this

1. List three safety features in cars that help to reduce the force on a passenger in a collision. **(3 marks)**

2. Explain how a seatbelt works. **(3 marks)**
3. You jump off a high wall. Explain why you should allow your knees to bend when you land. **(3 marks)**

Work and power

Work

Work is the amount of energy transferred, and is measured in joules (J).
The work done by a force is calculated using this formula:

work done (J) = force (N) × distance moved in the direction of the force (m)

$$E = F \times d$$

The E stands for energy.

The distance moved must be in the same direction as the force.

Power

Power is the rate of doing work (how fast energy is transferred). Power is measured in watts (W). 1 watt is 1 joule of energy being transferred every second.

$$\text{power (W)} = \frac{\text{work done (J)}}{\text{time taken (s)}}$$

$$P = \frac{E}{t}$$

Don't get work and power mixed up. Remember:

Work = energy transferred, measured in joules.

Power = *rate* of energy transfer, measured in watts.

Worked example

Dan uses a force of 100 N to push a box across the floor. He pushes it for 3 m. Calculate the work done.

Work = 100 N × 3 m
= 300 J

Worked example

Dan takes 5 seconds to push the box across the floor. Calculate his power.

$$\text{Power} = \frac{300\text{ J}}{5\text{ s}}$$
$$= 60\text{ W}$$

Now try this

1. Sam lifts a box onto a 1.5 metre high shelf. The box weighs 50 N.
   (a) Calculate the work done. **(3 marks)**
   (b) It takes Sam 2 seconds to lift the box. Calculate the power. **(3 marks)**

2. Joe does 60 000 J of work dragging a sledge for 10 minutes. Calculate his power. **(3 marks)**

Potential and kinetic energy

Gravitational potential energy

Gravitational potential energy is the energy stored in an object because it is in a high position.

On Earth, the gravitational field strength is 10 N/kg.

$$\text{gravitational potential energy (J)} = \text{mass (kg)} \times \text{gravitational field strength (N/kg)} \times \text{vertical height (m)}$$

$$GPE = m \times g \times h$$

Kinetic energy

Kinetic energy is the energy stored in moving objects.

$$\text{kinetic energy (J)} = \frac{1}{2} \times \text{mass (kg)} \times \text{velocity}^2 \ (\text{m/s})^2$$

$$KE = \frac{1}{2} \times m \times v^2$$

Don't forget to square the velocity. v^2 means $v \times v$

Worked example

A 1200 kg car is travelling at 25 m/s. Calculate the kinetic energy.

$$KE = \frac{1}{2} \times 1200\,\text{kg} \times 25\,(\text{m/s})^2$$

$$= 375\,000\,\text{J}$$

Conservation of energy

Energy cannot be created or destroyed. It can only be transferred from one form to another.

The roller coaster will eventually stop, as some of the kinetic and potential energy is transferred to thermal energy through friction and air resistance.

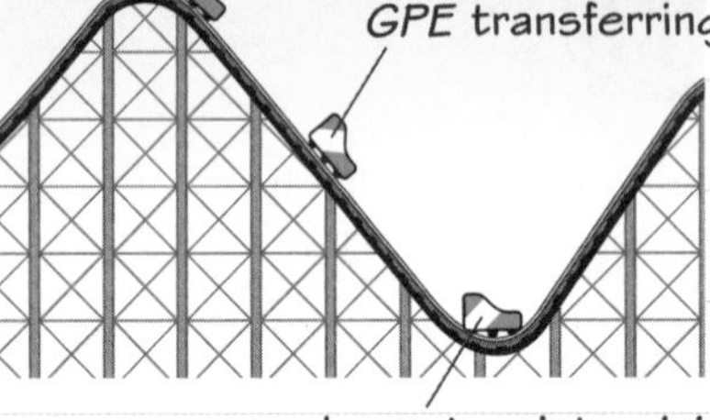

Now try this

1. Anita lifts a box onto a shelf. The box has a mass of 0.5 kg, and the shelf is 2 m from the floor.
   (a) Calculate the gravitational potential energy of the box. **(3 marks)**
   (b) The box falls off the shelf. Explain what its kinetic energy will be just before it hits the floor. **(2 marks)**
2. Ali and his bike together have a mass of 45 kg. Calculate the kinetic energy when he is cycling at 10 m/s. **(3 marks)**

EXAM ALERT!

More than nine out of ten students did not get any marks when answering a question on this subject in a recent exam paper. Remember that the work done to move an object to a higher position is the energy transferred to it. So the work done is the same as the amount of gravitational potential energy the object has in its new position.

Students have struggled with exam questions similar to this - **be prepared!**

Physics extended writing 2

Worked example

Describe three different safety devices in cars, and explain how they work. Use ideas about forces and momentum in your answer. **(6 marks)**

Sample answer 1

Seat belts stop you hitting the dashboard if the car crashes. Air bags stop the driver hitting their face on the steering wheel. Crumple zones crumple when the car crashes, so the rest of the car comes to a stop more slowly.

This is a basic answer. It correctly mentions the three safety devices that you need to know about, and there are basic statements about how each one works.

The question asked for ideas about momentum in the answer, and momentum is not mentioned at all. The statement about crumple zones increasing the time for the rest of the car to come to a stop is correct, and is part of the explanation involving momentum, but there is more to the explanation than this.

Sample answer 2

A moving car and the people inside it all have momentum. When the car crashes and comes to a stop the momentum changes to zero because of the force from the crash. The force is greater when the momentum changes faster.

Cars have crumple zones at the front which get squashed when there is a crash. This means the rest of the car takes longer to come to a stop so the momentum changes more slowly and there is a smaller force.

Seat belts hold the person in their seat and stop them flying forwards when the car crashes. The seat belt stretches a bit, so the person takes even longer to stop than the car and so the force is less. Air bags do the same thing – they are a bit squashy, which means people's heads take longer to slow down and they do not bang their heads on the steering wheel or dashboard.

This is an excellent answer. It contains all the scientific points to answer the question, and it is also well organised. This student has started out by explaining how changing momentum is connected to the forces in a crash, and then explained how each of the three safety features helps to slow down the change in momentum.

Now try this

1. Explain why a falling object on the Earth reaches a terminal velocity, and why this does not happen to a falling object on the Moon. **(6 marks)**

Physics extended writing 3

Worked example

Motorway signs often carry safety messages such as 'Don't drive tired' or 'Don't drink and drive'.

Explain how the stopping distance of a car may be affected if a driver is tired or has been drinking alcohol, and explain three other factors that can also affect stopping distances. **(6 marks)**

Sample answer 1

If the driver is tired or has been drinking their reaction time will be slower. This will make their stopping distance longer.

Other things that can make the stopping distance longer are if the car is going faster or if it has poor brakes or if the road is slippery.

This is a basic answer. The answer does explain that a tired or drunk driver will have a longer reaction time, but this part of the answer would have been better if it had explained that this will affect the thinking distance.

The answer does mention three other factors, but does not explain why these will affect the stopping distance or whether they will affect the thinking distance or the braking distance.

Sample answer 2

A tired driver or one who has been drinking alcohol will take longer to react to a danger ahead, so the thinking distance will be longer, this is the distance the car travels while the driver is deciding that they need to press on the brakes, and the other part of the stopping distance is the braking distance which is how far the car travels while it is slowing down.

If the car is travelling faster it will go further while the driver is thinking, and it will also travel further while the brakes are slowing it down so the thinking distance and the braking distance will both be longer so the stopping distance will be longer.

It takes longer to slow down a heavier car because it has more momentum and so the braking distance will be longer if the car is heavier but the thinking distance won't change but the stopping distance goes up because the braking distance has gone up.

Slippery roads might make the car skid or the tyres lose their grip so the braking distance would go up but the thinking distance would not.

This is an excellent answer, and it explains everything asked for in the question. It may not get full marks because of the way it is written. The sentences are very long (each paragraph is just one sentence), which makes it more difficult to read.

Now try this

1. The carriages on this roller coaster are moved to the top of the first rise using an electric motor. No further energy is supplied to the carriages after that.

Describe the energy changes during a roller coaster ride, and explain why the carriages have almost slowed to a stop by the end of the ride. **(6 marks)**

Isotopes

Atoms

Atoms are made up of protons, neutrons and electrons. The protons and neutrons are in the nucleus of the atom, and the electrons move around the outside.

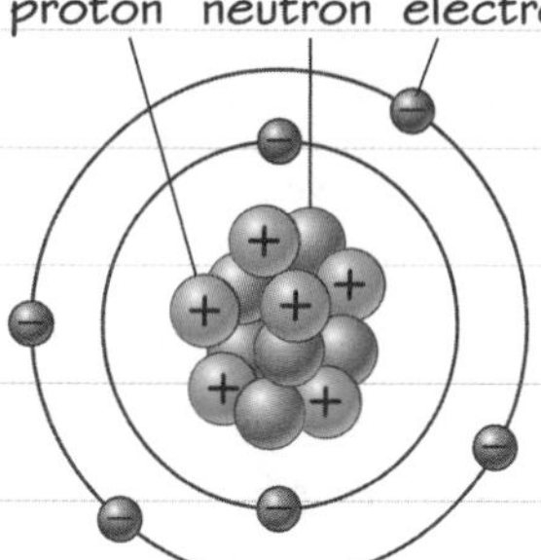

Describing atoms

All the atoms of a particular element have the same number of protons. The number of protons in each atom of an element is called the atomic number, or proton number.

The total number of protons and neutrons in an atom is the mass number, or nucleon number.

The atomic number and mass number of an element can be shown like this:

mass number — $^{16}_{8}O$ — atomic number

Worked example

The symbol represents an atom of sodium.

$^{23}_{11}Na$

Explain what these numbers tell you about an atom of sodium.

Remember: The mass number is always more than the atomic number (except hydrogen where both numbers are 1).
The top number in the symbol is the total number of particles in the nucleus.

The atomic number means sodium has 11 protons in the nucleus. The mass number says the number of protons plus neutrons is 23, so the number of neutrons is 23 − 11 = 12.

EXAM ALERT!

Only about half of all students answering a similar question in an exam paper recently got full marks. You need to learn the parts of an atom and how they are represented.

Students have struggled with exam questions similar to this - **be prepared!** ResultsPlus

Isotopes

Atoms of a particular element always have the same number of protons, but they can have different numbers of neutrons. Atoms with the same number of protons but different numbers of neutrons are isotopes of the same element.

lithium-6		lithium-7	
$^{6}_{3}Li$	3 protons 3 neutrons 3 electrons	$^{7}_{3}Li$	3 protons 4 neutrons 3 electrons

Now try this

target G-D

1. An atom of boron (B) has 5 protons and 6 neutrons.
   (a) State the atomic number of boron. **(1 mark)**
   (b) State the mass number of boron. **(1 mark)**
   (c) Show the atomic number and mass number as a symbol for the isotope. **(1 mark)**

target D-C

2. These are the symbols for two isotopes of nitrogen.

   nitrogen-14 $^{14}_{7}N$ nitrogen-15 $^{15}_{7}N$

   Describe the similarities and differences between the two isotopes. **(3 marks)**

Ionising radiation

Some types of radiation can cause atoms to lose electrons and become ions. An ion is an atom that has an electrical charge because it has gained or lost electrons (see also page 40).

Alpha, beta or gamma

Some elements are radioactive. Their nuclei are unstable. This means that they may decay (change) by emitting radiation. Unstable nuclei can emit alpha, beta or gamma radiation. All these are forms of ionising radiation.

Beta particles are electrons emitted from the *nucleus* of unstable atoms. An atom that emits beta particles still has all its usual electrons moving around the nucleus.

- An alpha particle is equivalent to a helium nucleus. It has two protons and two neutrons (but no electrons), so it has an electrical charge of +2.
- A beta particle is an electron, so it has a negative electrical charge of −1.
- Gamma radiation is a form of electromagnetic radiation. Gamma rays are waves, not particles. This means that they do not have a charge.

Comparing the properties

The different types of radiation have different properties. An alpha particle is more likely to ionise an atom than a gamma ray, but a gamma ray will travel further.

(α) alpha particles
- will travel a few centimetres in air
- very ionising
- can be stopped by a sheet of paper

(β) beta particles
- will travel a few metres in air
- moderately ionising
- can be stopped by 3 mm thick aluminium

(γ) gamma rays
- will travel a few kilometres in air
- weakly ionising
- need thick lead to stop them

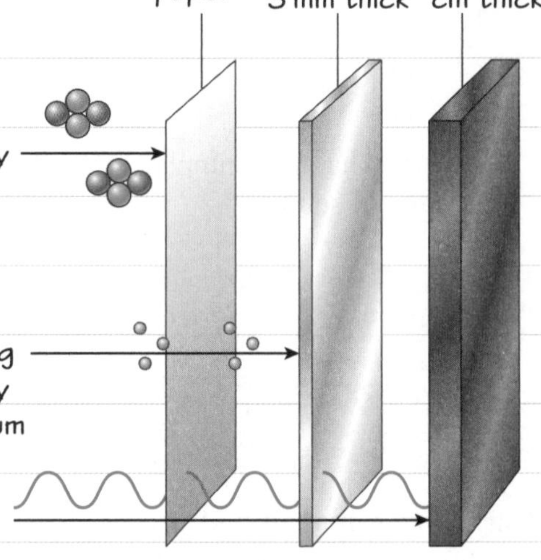

EXAM ALERT!

You need to learn the properties of the different types of radiation. About seven out of ten students did not achieve any marks on a question on this subject in a recent exam.

Students have struggled with exam questions similar to this - **be prepared!** ResultsPlus

Worked example

Write down the three types of radiation in order of

(a) how penetrating they are, starting with the most penetrating

(a) gamma, beta, alpha

(b) their ionising power, starting with the most ionising.

(b) alpha, beta, gamma

Remember – gamma rays are the *most* penetrating and the *least* ionising.

Now try this

target G-D

1. (a) Describe an alpha particle. **(2 marks)**

(b) Describe a beta particle. **(2 marks)**

2. State the type of radiation that:

(a) will travel the furthest through air **(1 mark)**

(b) is most likely to ionise an atom that it meets. **(1 mark)**

Nuclear reactions

Atoms emit alpha, beta or gamma radiation in radioactive decay. Other kinds of nuclear reaction are fission and fusion (see page 93). All nuclear reactions can be sources of energy.

Fission

In a fission reaction, a large unstable nucleus splits into two smaller ones. For example, a uranium-235 nucleus splits up when it absorbs a neutron. The fission of uranium-235 produces two daughter nuclei, two or more neutrons, and also releases energy.

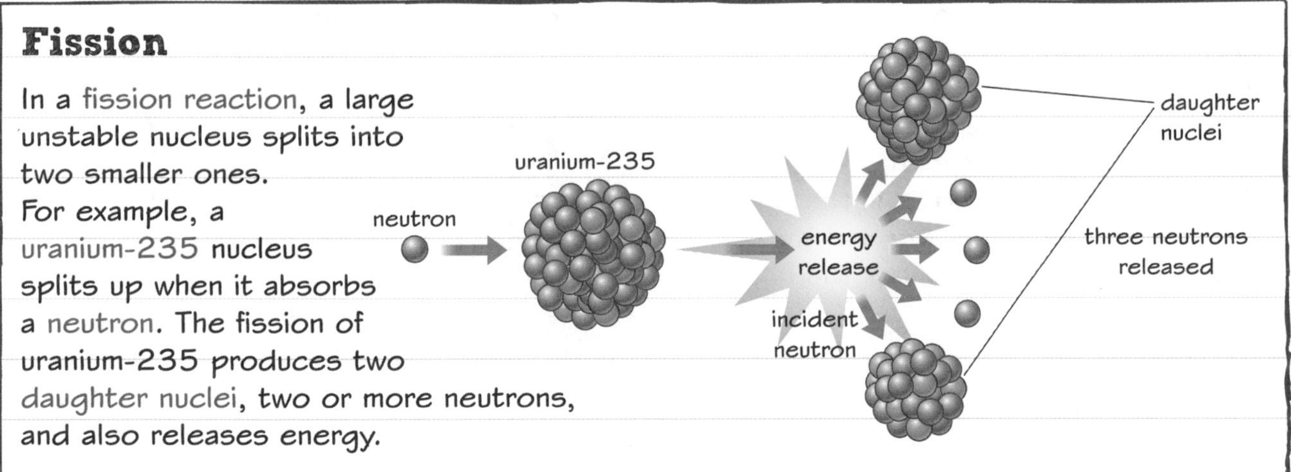

Chain reactions

The neutrons released by the fission of U-235 may be absorbed by other nuclei. Each of these nuclei may undergo fission, and produce even more neutrons. This is called a chain reaction. If a chain reaction is not controlled there will be a nuclear explosion.

Nuclear reactors make use of controlled chain reactions (see page 92).

Worked example

Describe how a chain reaction can be controlled.

A chain reaction can be controlled by using a different material to absorb some of the neutrons. This slows the reaction down because there are fewer neutrons to cause more nuclei to fission.

Controlled chain reactions

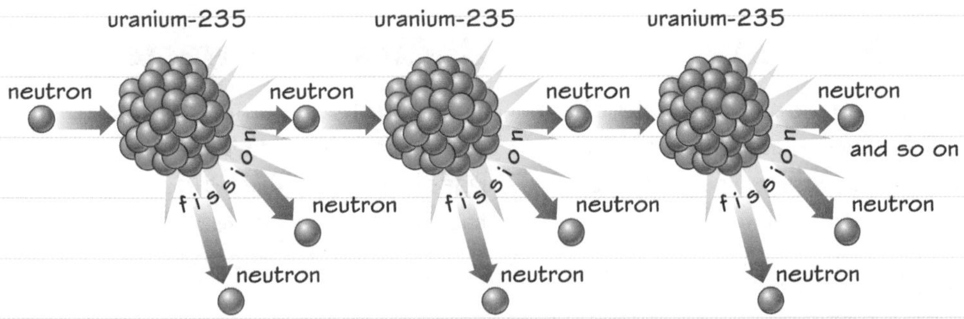

Two of the neutrons are absorbed by other materials. Only one neutron from each fission can cause other fission. This is a controlled chain reaction.

Now try this

1. Name three different types of nuclear reaction. **(3 marks)**
2. Name the particle that causes a fission reaction in uranium-235. **(1 mark)**

target D-C

3. Describe what happens in a chain reaction. **(3 marks)**

Nuclear power

Nuclear power stations

Nuclear power stations use nuclear fuels such as uranium-235. The fuel is made into fuel rods. A reactor core is made of a material called a moderator. Fuel rods and control rods fit into holes in the moderator. The moderator and the control rods help to control the chain reaction.

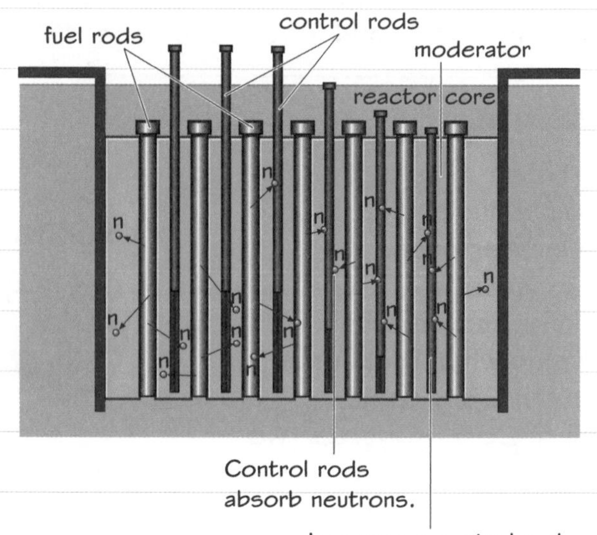

Controlling the reaction

The neutrons produced by fission reactions are moving very fast. The moderator slows them down so that they are more likely to be absorbed by another U-235 nucleus and cause another fission reaction.

The moderator does not slow down or speed up the rate of the chain reaction. The control rods are moved in or out to do that.

Worked example

Explain how the control rods work in a nuclear power station.

The control rods **absorb** neutrons. If the control rods are pushed down into the core, more neutrons are absorbed and the chain reaction slows down. If they are pulled out, fewer neutrons are absorbed and the chain reaction speeds up.

Generating electricity

Thermal (heat) energy released by the chain reaction is used to turn water into steam. The steam makes a turbine spin, and the turbine drives a generator.

Nuclear power stations produce steam and use it to turn turbines in the same way as fossil-fuelled power stations do. The difference is the way the heat is produced.

Radioactive waste

The daughter nuclei produced in the fission reaction are radioactive. The neutrons passing through the core can form other radioactive isotopes. This radioactive waste must be disposed of safely.

Now try this

1. Describe how the thermal energy produced by fission reactions is used in a nuclear power station. **(3 marks)**

2. Explain what the following parts of a nuclear reactor do:
   (a) control rods **(3 marks)**
   (b) moderator. **(3 marks)**

Fusion – our future?

Fusion

Nuclear fusion happens when small nuclei join to form larger ones. Like all nuclear reactions, fusion reactions release energy.

Isotopes of hydrogen combine in the Sun to form helium. The energy released by these reactions is what makes the Sun shine.

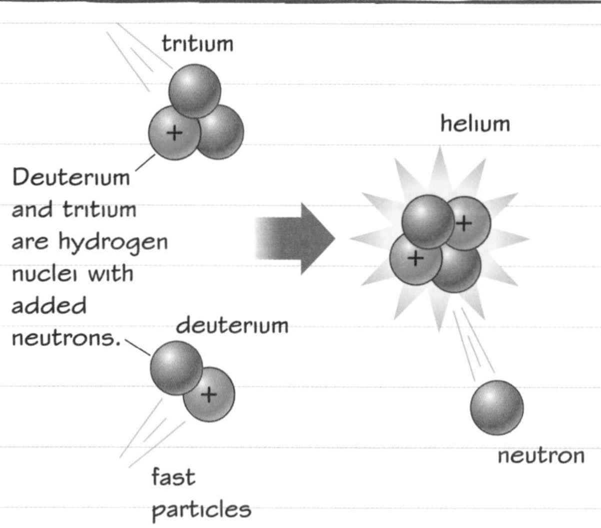

Worked example

Name the type of nuclear reaction that occurs:

(a) in a nuclear power station

(a) fission

(b) in the Sun.

(b) fusion

Nuclear fission is the splitting up of large, unstable nuclei to form smaller daughter nuclei.
Nuclear fusion is the joining of small nuclei to make larger ones.

'Cold fusion'

Fusion reactions only happen at very high temperatures and pressures. This makes them difficult to use for generating electricity. In 1989 two scientists announced that they had made nuclear fusion happen at 50°C. This became known as 'cold fusion'. Their results have not been accepted because they could not be validated.

Scientists make a new discovery.

They describe their method and results in a paper, which they send to an academic journal.

The editor sends the paper to other scientists for checking. This is called peer review.

The journal publishes the paper, and other scientists try to reproduce the results.

The discovery is validated if the results can be reproduced.

The scientific process.

Now try this

target E-C

1. Describe the difference between fission and fusion. **(2 marks)**
2. Describe two things that need to happen before a new scientific theory is accepted by the scientific community. **(2 marks)**

Changing ideas

Ionising radiation is radiation that can remove electrons from atoms and form ions. Alpha, beta and gamma radiation are all forms of ionising radiation. Ionising radiation can damage tissues in the body, causing radiation burns (reddened skin), or may cause mutations in DNA, which can kill cells or cause cancer.

Precautions

People using radioactive material take precautions to make sure they stay safe.

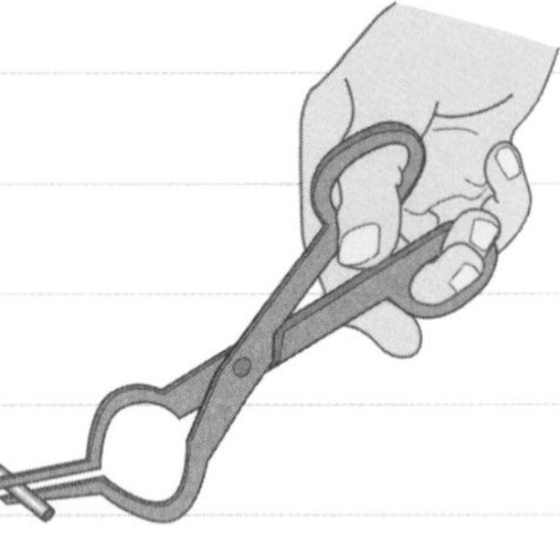

The radioactive source is being moved using tongs to keep it as far away from the person's hand as possible. The source is always kept pointing away from people.

Worked example

Explain two precautions that a radiation worker could take.

They could wear overalls to make sure radioactive particles do not get caught in their clothing.

They could wear breathing apparatus to make sure radioactive material does not get into their lungs.

Remember that if a question asks you to 'explain' something, you need to give a reason why something happens or something is done.

Changing ideas

When radioactivity was first discovered, scientists did not realise that it was harmful. Scientists using radioactivity suffered burns to their skin, but they did not realise that ionising radiation could cause cancer.	In the 1920s scientists began to see a link between working with radioactivity and the chances of getting cancer. Scientists also now know about DNA and that some changes to DNA can be caused by ionising radiation.	Today scientists have discovered how to work with radioactivity safely, including the amount of radioactivity we can be exposed to without danger.

If an exam question asks you to 'suggest' something, it means you may not have learned the answer directly. You need to use your scientific knowledge to help you to work out the answer.

Worked example

Suggest two reasons why ideas about the hazards of radioactivity have changed.

Scientists have gathered evidence about exposure to radioactivity and illness, and scientists have carried out experiments to find out *how* radioactivity is harmful.

Now try this

1. Name three forms of ionising radiation. **(3 marks)**
2. Explain how ionising radiation can cause cancer. **(2 marks)**
3. Describe one precaution that a teacher using a radioactive source in class should take. **(1 mark)**

Nuclear waste

Waste from nuclear power stations is radioactive and must be disposed of safely. Hospitals and research laboratories can also produce some radioactive waste. There are different ways of disposing of waste, depending on how radioactive it is.

Types of waste

- High level waste (HLW) is very radioactive. It is sealed into glass and stored until it has become less radioactive (after about 50 years, when it becomes ILW).
- Intermediate level waste (ILW) remains radioactive for tens of thousands of years. It is stored in steel and concrete containers.
- Low level waste (LLW) includes waste from hospitals, and clothing and cleaning materials from nuclear power stations. It is buried in special landfill sites.

Worked example

Suggest two ways of disposing of high and intermediate level waste. State one disadvantage of each method.

It could be fired into space, but radioactive material would be spread over a wide area if there was an accident during launch.

It could be dumped at sea, but radioactive materials could get into the oceans if the storage containers leaked.

Nuclear waste could also be stored underground. This would have to be done in an area that is not likely to have earthquakes.

Nuclear power

There are advantages and disadvantages to using nuclear energy to generate electricity.

- ✓ Nuclear power stations do not produce carbon dioxide, so they do not contribute to climate change.
- ✓ Supplies of nuclear fuel will last longer than supplies of fossil fuels.
- ✗ It is difficult and expensive to store nuclear waste safely.
- ✗ An accident in a nuclear power station can spread radioactive material over a large area.
- ✗ Many people think that nuclear power is dangerous, and do not want new nuclear power stations to be built.

However, construction processes produce carbon dioxide, so carbon dioxide will be added to the atmosphere when the power station is built and when fuel rods are made.

Nuclear power stations do not make the local area more radioactive when they are working properly. This only happens if there is an accident.

Now try this

target G-E

1. State one advantage and one disadvantage of using nuclear power to generate electricity. **(2 marks)**
2. Explain why nuclear waste should not be buried in an area where there might be earthquakes. **(2 marks)**

Half-life

The activity of a radioactive source is the number of atoms that decay every second. The unit for activity is the becquerel (Bq). When an atom decays it emits radiation but changes into a more stable isotope.

Unstable atoms

The activity of a source depends on how many unstable atoms there are in a sample, and on the particular isotope. As more and more atoms in a sample decay, there are fewer unstable ones left, so the activity decreases. The half-life of a radioactive isotope is the time it takes for half of the unstable atoms to decay. This is also the time for the activity to go down by half.

Be careful when you are writing about half-life. It is not the time for an atom to decay – it is the time for half of the atoms *in a sample* to decay.

Worked example

The half-life of caesium-137 is 30 years. How long does it take for the activity of a sample to change from 100 Bq to 25 Bq?

After 30 years (1 half-life) the activity will be 50 Bq.

After 60 years (2 half-lives) the activity will be 25 Bq.

It will take 60 years.

Worked example

The graph shows how the activity of a sample changes over 24 hours. What is the half-life of the sample?

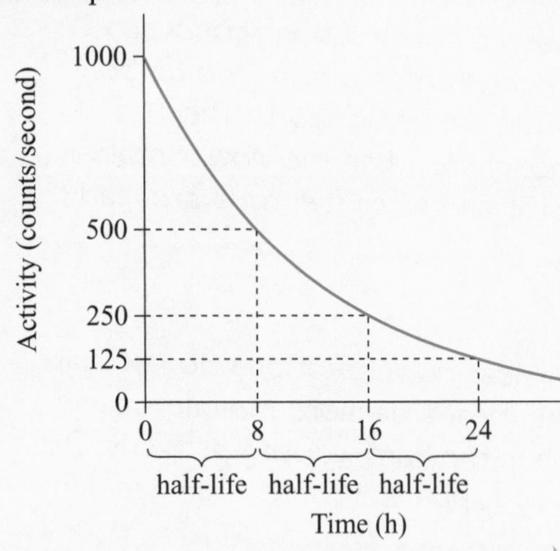

Activity at time 0 = 1000 Bq

Half of this is 500 Bq. The activity is 500 Bq at 8 hours.

The half-life is 8 hours.

EXAM ALERT!

About two-fifths of all students did not achieve full marks on a similar question in a recent exam. Remember that the half-life is the amount of time it takes for the activity to halve.

Students have struggled with exam questions similar to this - **be prepared!** ResultsPlus

Models for decay

Radioactive decay is a random process. You can model how the atoms in a sample decay using other random processes, such as flipping a coin or throwing a dice.

Now try this

1. Explain what 'half-life' means. **(1 mark)**
2. The activity of a source is 60 Bq. The activity is 15 Bq four hours later. What is the half-life of the source? **(3 marks)**

Uses of radiation

Background radiation

We are always exposed to ionising radiation. This is called background radiation. This radiation comes from different sources, as shown in the pie chart.

Radon is a radioactive gas that is produced when uranium in rocks decays. The radon can build up in houses and other buildings. The amount of radon gas varies from place to place, because it depends on the type of rock in the area.

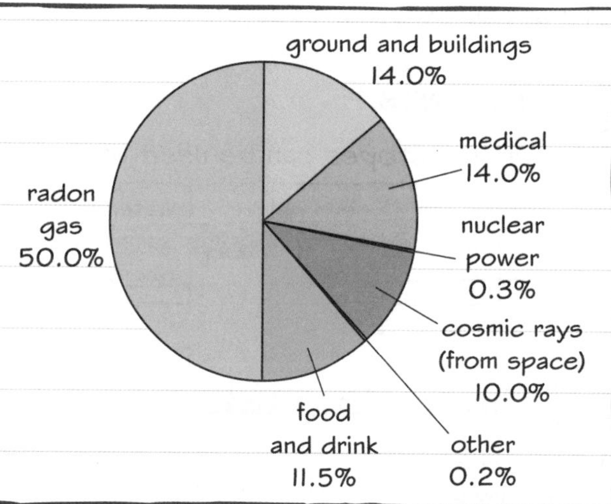

Radiation in hospitals

Radiation is used in hospitals to:

- Kill cancer cells – beams of gamma rays can be directed at cancer cells to kill them.
- Sterilise surgical instruments – gamma rays can be used to sterilize plastic instruments which cannot be sterilized by heating.
- Diagnose cancer – a tracer solution containing gamma radiation is injected into the body and taken up by cells which are growing abnormally. The places in the body where the tracer collects are detected with a 'gamma camera'.

Irradiating food

Worked example

Explain why gamma rays are used to irradiate food.

It makes the food safer to eat, and makes it last longer.

Don't get 'irradiated' and 'radioactive' mixed up. Irradiated food is not radioactive.

Bacteria on food eventually causes it to **decompose**, and some bacteria may cause food poisoning. **Irradiating** the food with gamma rays kills bacteria and any other organisms in it. This makes the food safer to eat. The food can also be stored for longer before it goes off.

Now try this

1. (a) Name the main source of background radiation in the UK. **(1 mark)**
   (b) Name three other sources of background radiation. **(3 marks)**

2. Explain how gamma rays can be used:
   (a) to detect cancer **(3 marks)**
   (b) to treat cancer. **(2 marks)**

More uses of radiation

Here are three other uses of radiation.

Tracers

Radioactive isotopes can be used to find leaks in pipes.

A gamma source is added to the water. → Water containing the gamma source escapes where there is a leak. → A detector above the ground detects higher levels of gamma radiation.

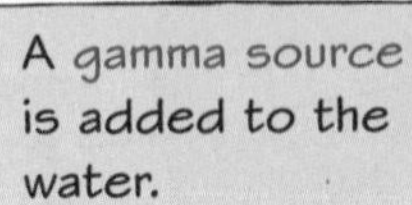

Controlling thickness

If the paper is too thick, not as many beta particles get through. → The rollers press together harder to make the paper thinner.

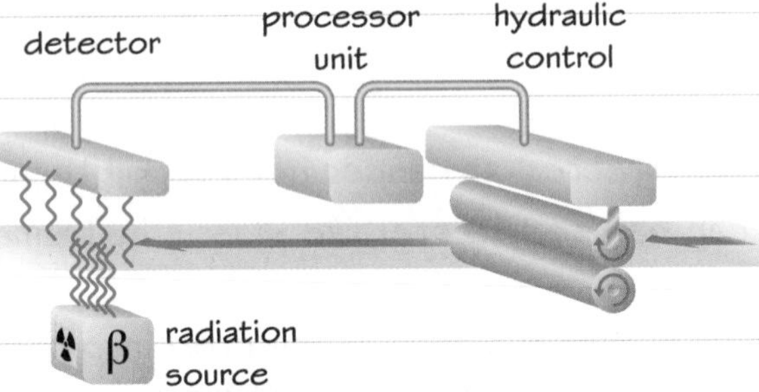

Beta particles being used to control the thickness of paper.

Worked example

Explain why beta particles are used to control the thickness of paper.

Alpha particles would not go through the paper at all. Gamma rays would pass through the paper too easily, and the amount getting through would hardly change with small changes in the thickness of the paper.

3 Smoke alarms

Smoke alarms contain a source of alpha radiation.

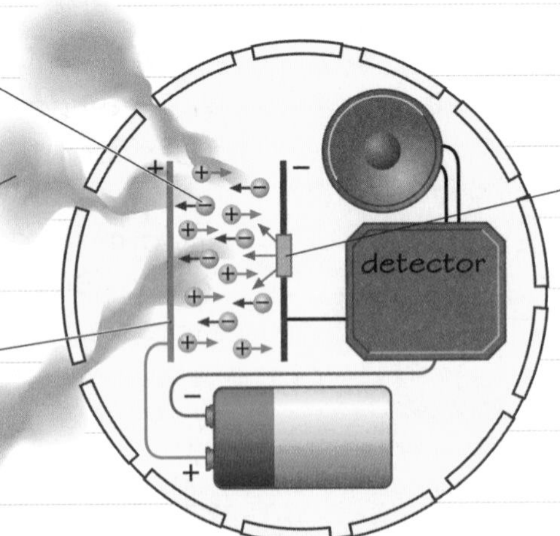

Alpha particles from the source ionise the air between two plates and allow a current to flow.
Smoke absorbs some of the alpha particles.
This reduces the size of the current between the plates and the alarm sounds.
detector
Source of radiation gives off a constant stream of alpha particles.

Now try this

1. Look at the diagram showing paper being made. Describe what will happen if the paper in the top diagram is too thin. **(2 marks)**
2. Explain how a smoke detector works. **(4 marks)**

Physics extended writing 4

Worked example

The diagram shows a machine used to produce paper. A source of beta radiation is used to monitor the thickness of the paper.

Explain why beta radiation is used for this purpose, and how the machine produces paper of a constant thickness.

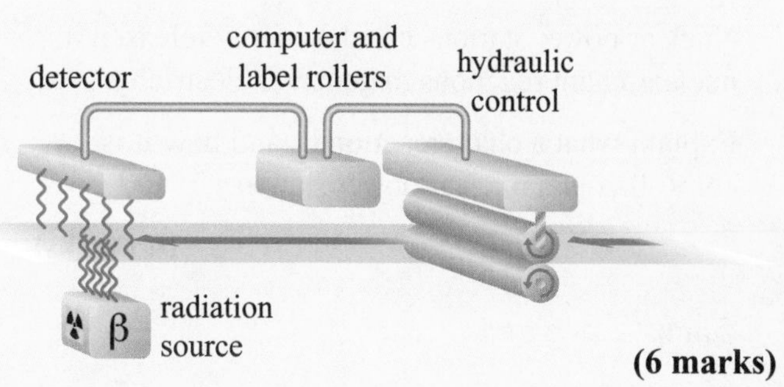

(6 marks)

Sample answer 1

Beta radiation is used because it goes through the paper. If the paper is too thick a lot of radiation gets through it and the rollers press harder to make the paper thinner. The opposite happens if the paper is too thin.

This is a basic answer. The first sentence is correct, although this is only part of the explanation for using beta radiation. The part of the answer explaining how the machine works is incorrect – less radiation would get through if the paper was too thick.

This student has not tried to explain what would happen if the paper was too thin. If they had written this part of the explanation out fully, they might have spotted the mistake they made earlier.

Always read through your work to check you have got your facts right. If you make a mistake, cross it out so the examiner knows which bit should be marked.

Sample answer 2

Beta radiation is used instead of alpha because alpha would not go through the paper at all. Beta is used instead of gamma because gamma would go through the paper very easily, and small differences in the thickness might not make much difference to how much gets through.

If the paper is too thin, more beta radiation will get through it and get to the detector. The computer changes the force on the rollers so they do not press so hard. If the paper is too thick not much radiation will get to the detector and the computer will tell the rollers to press harder and make the paper thinner.

This is an excellent answer. It explains why alpha and gamma radiation are not suitable, and also explains clearly how the machine works.

Now try this

1. These symbols represent carbon-12, carbon-14 and nitrogen-14.

   $^{12}_{6}C$ $^{14}_{6}C$ $^{14}_{7}N$

   Compare the atoms described by these symbols. **(6 marks)**

If a question asks you to compare something you need to discuss the differences and the similarities.

Physics extended writing 5

Worked example

Nuclear power stations use the energy released in nuclear chain reactions to generate electricity.

Explain what a chain reaction is, and how it is controlled in a nuclear power station.

(6 marks)

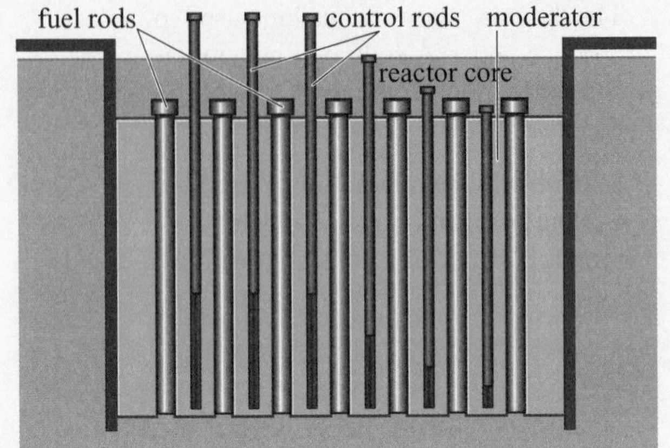

Sample answer 1

A chain reaction happens when uranium splits up and makes two smaller atoms and some neutrons. The neutrons can make other atoms split up, and those give out more neutrons, and so on. This is controlled in a power station using a moderator and control rods.

This is a basic answer. It describes a chain reaction quite well, although this description would be better if correct scientific words such as nucleus, isotope and fission were included. However it does not answer the second part of the question at all. This answer would get no marks for mentioning the moderator or the control rods, as these items are shown in the diagram.
Remember to answer *all* parts of the question!

Sample answer 2

When fission happens to uranium-235 it splits up to make two daughter nuclei and also produces some neutrons. These neutrons can hit other nuclei and make them fission as well, and they produce more neutrons, and so on. This is a chain reaction.

In a nuclear reactor the moderator slows down the neutrons to make sure they cause more fission reactions. This makes sure the reaction keeps going. There are also control rods. These absorb neutrons, so when they are pushed into the core they make fewer reactions and when they are pulled out they let more reactions happen. The best way is when only one neutron from a fission can start another one, so the reactions happen at the same rate.

This is an excellent answer. It explains what a chain reaction is clearly, and also explains why the moderator and the control rods are needed in a nuclear reactor.

Now try this

1. Radioactive isotopes can produce alpha, beta and gamma radiation. Describe the similarities and differences between these types of radiation. **(6 marks)**

Balancing equations

You can represent what happens in a chemical reaction using equations. Equations can be in words or they can use symbols for the elements and compounds.

If you are asked for a word equation, don't be tempted to use the formulae as a short-cut.

hydrogen + oxygen → water

$2H_2 + O_2 \rightarrow 2H_2O$

There are 2 oxygen atoms here as well, because there are 2 molecules of water, each with 1 oxygen atom.

There are 2 oxygen atoms here, joined into 1 molecule.

This is a **balanced equation**: it has the same number of hydrogen and oxygen atoms on each side of the → sign.

Remember:

- Count the number of different atoms on each side of the → sign to check if your equation is balanced.
- The big number in front of a formula tells you how many molecules of a covalent substance, units of an ionic substance or atoms of a metal there are.
- You must not try to balance an equation by changing the formulae of the compounds! You can only add more molecules.
- You may be asked to include state symbols in your equation – (s) for solid, (l) for liquid, (g) for gas and (aq) for a substance in solution.

Worked example

Lithium (Li) reacts with water to form lithium hydroxide (LiOH) and hydrogen gas. Write a balanced equation to represent this reaction. Include state symbols.

$2Li(s) + 2H_2O(l) \rightarrow 2LiOH(aq) + H_2(g)$

You are expected to know the symbols and formulae for some of the common substances, such as water and hydrogen gas.

Start by writing down all the formulae and state symbols:

$Li(s) + H_2O(l) \rightarrow LiOH(aq) + H_2(g)$

Count the atoms on each side. You can easily see there are more hydrogen atoms on the right, so you need to add more on the left. You can only do this by putting a 2 in front of the water.

$Li(s) + 2H_2O(l) \rightarrow LiOH(aq) + H_2(g)$

Now there is more oxygen on the left than on the right, so increase the number on the right by putting a 2 in front of LiOH.

$Li(s) + 2H_2O(l) \rightarrow 2LiOH(aq) + H_2(g)$

Now you need to increase the number of lithium atoms on the left, so put a 2 in front of Li.

$2Li(s) + 2H_2O(l) \rightarrow 2LiOH(aq) + H_2(g)$

Count the atoms on each side again to check – the equation is now balanced.

Practical work

The Edexcel Additional Science course includes suggestions for many different investigations. By the time you sit your exams you will have completed a Controlled Assessment, based on one or more of these investigations. But you could also be asked questions about any of these practicals in the exam.

This revision guide includes a brief summary of a method that could be used for each of the suggested investigations. The worked examples below should help with other kinds of questions.

Questions based on practical work could include:

- providing a hypothesis, and justifying it
- writing a method for an investigation
- explaining how to control variables
- drawing a graph to show some results
- writing a conclusion based on results given in the exam paper
- evaluating a method or a conclusion.

Worked example

A student is investigating the relationship between potential difference, current and resistance. Write a hypothesis and method for this investigation.

Hypothesis: if the resistance in a circuit is increased, the current will be smaller for a particular potential difference. This is because a higher resistance means it is harder for a current to flow through the component.

This is a good hypothesis, because it shows that the student has recalled what they have learned about current, potential difference and resistance.

Method: Set up a circuit with an ammeter in series with a resistor, and with a power pack or battery to provide a constant potential difference. Measure the current. Add another resistor to the circuit and measure the current again. Keep doing this until the current has been measured for 5 different resistances of the circuit.

You should usually have at least 5 data points if you want to draw a graph of your results.

Plot a graph of resistance against current to see the relationship between the two variables.

You must describe a method in the correct order. It may help to jot down some ideas in a blank space on your exam paper to help you to get your ideas in order. If the question asks you to explain the method, remember to say *why* each step is needed.

Other questions on planning

Other questions on the planning part of a practical could include asking you to:

- explain the apparatus needed
- identify the variables to be controlled and explain how they can be controlled
- identify risks and describe how to manage them.

Dealing with evidence

Worked example

The graph shows the results of an investigation to find out how the rate of anaerobic respiration in yeast depends on the concentration of glucose. The rate of respiration was measured by finding the volume of carbon dioxide produced in 10 minutes. Complete the graph by drawing a line of best fit.

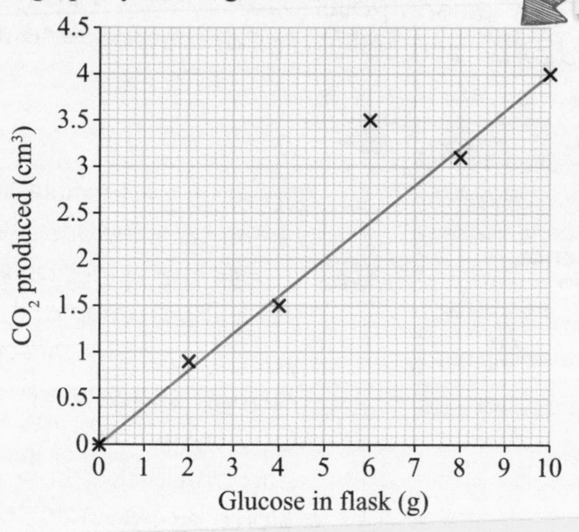

A 'line of best fit' can be a straight line or it can be a smooth curve. In this question, the points are along a straight line (apart from the one that obviously does not fit the pattern), so draw a straight line using a ruler.

This is a good answer because the student has drawn a single straight line through most of the points. You will not get any marks for a graph question if you join each of the points using straight lines. Try to include as many points as possible on your line or curve, but ignore any that are obviously not following the pattern of most of your results.

A result that does not fit the pattern is an **anomalous result**. The student has probably made a mistake when measuring or recording the result for 6 g of glucose.

Do not include anomalous results when you are working out means, or when you are drawing lines or curves of best fit.

Conclusions and evaluations

Worked example

A student investigating respiration in yeast had the following hypothesis: 'The rate of respiration will increase when the concentration of glucose increases.'

Look at the graph of their results (above).

(a) Write a conclusion for this investigation.

(a) The graph shows that the rate of respiration of the yeast increases when the concentration of glucose increases. The hypothesis was correct.

This would be a better answer if the conclusion described the shape of the graph in more detail. The graph is a straight line through the origin (0, 0), so the volume of CO_2 produced is proportional to the mass of glucose used. Proportional means that the CO_2 doubles if the glucose doubles.

(b) Evaluate the quality of the conclusion.

(b) All the points except one are close to the line of best fit. The result for 6 g of glucose was probably a mistake. The quality of the data could be improved by using several flasks with each mass of glucose and finding means (averages) of the results.

The conclusion may not apply if more glucose is used. Too much glucose might be bad for the yeast.

Many relationships are only true up to certain values of one of the variables. So you can only really say that your conclusion is valid for the range of the variables you have tested.

Final comments

Here are some other things to remember in your exam.

Read the question carefully. Underline important words in the question to help you to understand what you need to do. Using correct science is great, but no use if it does not actually answer the question!

Use the correct scientific words for things and don't be vague in your answers. For example, saying 'fossil fuels cause pollution' isn't specific enough. Saying *how* they cause pollution is better ('burning fossil fuels causes pollution because carbon dioxide and sulfur dioxide get into the air').

Know what the command words mean at the start of a question. If you are asked to 'explain' then you need to say what happens and how or why it happens. If a question asks you to 'compare' then you need to write down something about all the things you are comparing and how they are similar and different.

Write your name here

Surname | Other names

Edexcel GCSE — Centre Number — Candidate Number

Chemistry/Science

Unit C2: Discovering Chemistry

Foundation Tier

Time: 1 hour — Paper Reference **XXX**

You must have: Calculator, ruler — Total Marks

Instructions

- Use **black** ink or ball-point pen.
- **Fill in the boxes** at the top of this page with your name, centre number and candidate number.
- Answer **all** questions.
- Answer the questions in the spaces provided – *there may be more space than you need.*

Information

- The total mark for this paper is 60.
- The marks for **each** question are shown in brackets – *use this as a guide as to how much time to spend on each question.*
- Questions labelled with an **asterisk** (*) are ones where the quality of your written communication will be assessed – *you should take particular care with your spelling, punctuation and grammar, as well as the clarity of expression, on these questions.*

Advice

- Read each question carefully before you start to answer it.
- Keep an eye on the time.
- Try to answer every question.
- Check your answers if you have time at the end.

Turn over

P40176A

P 4 0 1 7 6 A 0 1 2 0

edexcel advancing learning, changing lives

Don't use a formula for chemical substances unless the question asks for it. For example, if your answer is carbon dioxide and you write C_2O by mistake (because carbon dioxide is CO_2), it won't be possible to tell that you knew the right answer.

Learn how to balance chemical equations. And remember that all the gases that take part in the reactions you need to know about for this course are diatomic (their formulae are: O_2, Cl_2, N_2, and so on).

Revise the investigations you have carried out during the course. You may be asked questions on practical work in the exam.

Show your working for calculation questions, even if you use a calculator. And don't forget to include the units with your final answer.

Using formula triangles

There will be a formula sheet in the exam, so you do not need to memorise equations, but you do need to be able to rearrange them.

If you cannot remember how to do this, you need to memorise the formula triangles given with formulae in this book. For example, $P = I \times V$ will be given in the exam paper. If you need to work out the voltage (V), cover up the V on the formula triangle. This will tell you that you need to divide P by I to get your answer.

$P = I \times V$ (given in exam)

This can be rearranged as:

$V = \frac{P}{I}$ or $I = \frac{P}{V}$

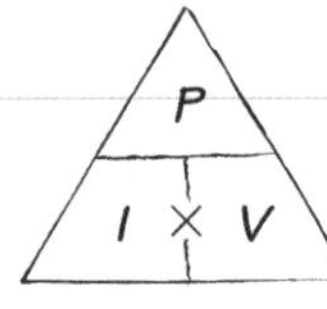

Answers

You will find some advice next to some of the answers. This is written in italics. It is not part of the mark scheme but just gives you a little more information.

Biology answers

3. Plant and animal cells

1. (**1** mark for each correct row)

Component	Found in plant cells?	Found in animal cells?	Function
cell wall	yes	no	gives cell a strong shape
cell membrane	yes	yes	controls what enters and leaves cell
chloroplasts	yes	no	where photosynthesis takes place and makes food
cytoplasm	yes	yes	to support other structures and where some reactions happen
mitochondria	yes	yes	where respiration releases energy
nucleus	yes	yes	contains DNA, which controls what is made and how the cell works
vacuole	yes	no	contains cell sap and helps to support plant when full

2. Only plant cells can photosynthesise/make their own food/are autotrophic. **(1)** Animals don't need chloroplasts because they get their food from eating other organisms/are heterotrophic. **(1)**
3. cell wall and vacuole; **(1)** cell wall helps provide support and vacuole keeps the cells rigid. **(1)**

4. Inside bacteria

1. **(a)** any two from: plasmid DNA; chromosomal DNA; flagellum (**1** each)
   (b) nucleus **(1)**
2. $5 \times 40 \times 0.05$ mm **(1)** = 10 mm/1 cm **(1)**

5. DNA

1. In the nucleus **(1)**
2. Any suitable sentences that give appropriate definitions, such as:
   (a) A gene is a short section of DNA that codes for a specific protein. **(1)**
   (b) DNA is a double helix molecule made of complementary bases. **(1)**
   (c) There are four bases in DNA: A, T, C and G. **(1)**
3. GCTA; **(1)** G always pairs with C and T always pairs with A. **(1)**

6. Genetic engineering

1. **(a)** bacterium **(1)**
   (b) because it contains the human gene for insulin **(1)**
2. an organism that has a gene in its DNA **(1)** that comes from another organism **(1)**
3. The gene for the characteristic is cut out of/is isolated from the DNA of an organism that normally has that characteristic. **(1)** The gene is inserted into the DNA of another organism **(1)** so that it produces its characteristic in the new organism. **(1)**

7. Mitosis

1. **(a)** two **(1)** **(b)** identical **(1)**
2. Bacteria that split in two to make more bacteria. **(1)** Plants that produce new plantlets that split from the parent plant when they are large enough to grow on their own. **(1)** *Other answers are possible here.*
3. In mitosis each chromosome is copied exactly **(1)** and when the cell divides each daughter cell gets one of the copies of each chromosome. **(1)**

8. Fertilisation and meiosis

1. **(a)** four **(1)** **(b)** one **(1)**
2. Any correct use of each word, such as: During fertilisation, a male haploid gamete and a female haploid gamete combine to form a diploid zygote. (**1** mark for each word correctly used, up to **4**)

9. Making clones

1. A clone has identical genes to another organism. **(1)** It can be produced by asexual reproduction. **(1)**
2. **(a)** Yes **(1)** because they will have the same genes as the GM parent goat including the human hormone gene. **(1)**
   (b) Any suitable answer, such as: could be very expensive because it takes many attempts to make the clones, or cloned goats may suffer more health problems than normal goats. **(1)**

10. Stem cells

1. **(a)** A stem cell can divide to produce many types of cell, but a body cell cannot. **(1)**
   (b) A differentiated cell is one that is specialised, such as a muscle cell. **(1)**
2. **(a)** Either: they are easier to extract, or they can produce more different kinds of cell. **(1)**
   (b) will make it easier to produce replacement cells than if adult stem cells are used **(1)**
3. **(a)** Embryos have to be destroyed when the stem cells are removed. **(1)**
   (b) Some people think it is wrong to do this because they believe it is the same as murder. **(1)**
4. Any stem cells placed in the body may turn into cancer cells that are harmful **(1)** rather than the healthy cells that the body needs. **(1)**

11. Protein synthesis

1. bases **(1)** amino acids **(1)**
2. a change in the base sequence in DNA/a gene **(1)**
3. They are made from different sequences of amino acids **(1)** and the order of the amino acids affects the shape of the protein. **(1)**

12. Enzymes

1. digestion **(1)** *There are other correct examples, but this is the only one you are expected to recall.*
2. any one from: DNA replication; protein synthesis **(1)** *There are other correct examples, but the ones given here are the only ones you are expected to recall.*
3. Enzymes are catalysts, which means they change the rate of reactions. **(1)** They are biological catalysts because they are found in living organisms. **(1)**

13. Enzyme action

1. temperature, **(1)** substrate concentration, **(1)** pH **(1)** *Don't use the term acidity instead of pH, because 'acidity' really only refers to part of the pH range.*
2. the temperature at which the rate of an enzyme controlled reaction is fastest **(1)**
3. **(a)** At low substrate concentrations, any increase in concentration produces a large increase in reaction rate. **(1)** As the substrate concentration increases, any increase in concentration produces a smaller increase in reaction rate until a point when no increase in reaction rate is produced/reaction rate levels out. **(1)**

(b) At low substrate concentration, there are not many substrate molecules to join with the enzyme molecules, so most enzyme molecules are free to combine with any additional substrate. **(1)** At high substrate concentration, almost all the enzyme molecules are joined with substrate molecules, so there aren't many free to combine with additional substrate. **(1)**

14. Explaining enzyme action

1. active site **(1)** product **(1)**
2. Enzymes are specific **(1)** because they only work with the substrate that has the right shape. **(1)**
3. The hypothesis shows how shape is important to how the enzyme works **(1)** so that only a substrate with the right shape will fit into the active site **(1)** and be changed in the reaction. **(1)**

15 and 16. Biology extended writing 1 and 2

Answers can be found on pages 110 and 111.

17. Aerobic respiration

1. oxygen **(1)** water **(1)**
2. Respiration releases energy, **(1)** which organisms need for life processes/growth, movement, etc. **(1)**
3. The concentration of oxygen is higher in the blood than in the tissues **(1)** because oxygen in the cells has been used in respiration/the blood contains oxygen collected in the lungs. **(1)**

18. Exercise

1. **(a)** count the number of breaths taken in one minute **(1)** *You could also use a breathing rate monitor if you have one.*
   (b) count the number of pulses measured at the wrist that happen in one minute **(1)** *You could also use a heart rate monitor if you have one.*
2. As exercise level increases/gets harder **(1)** the heart rate increases as well. **(1)** *It's not enough to say 'heart rate increases'. You need to link how heart rate changes as exercise level changes to get both marks.*
3. Any two from: Muscle cells are respiring faster because they are contracting faster. **(1)** Faster respiration needs more oxygen. **(1)** Faster breathing helps get oxygen into the blood more quickly. **(1)**

19. Anaerobic respiration

1. lactic acid **(1)**
2. It is the extra oxygen needed after exercise **(1)** some of which is used to break down lactic acid from anaerobic respiration. **(1)**
3. Running fast for 10 minutes will need more anaerobic respiration than running fast for 3 minutes. **(1)** More anaerobic respiration will produce more lactic acid, **(1)** which will need more oxygen to break it down. **(1)**

20. Photosynthesis

1. water **(1)** oxygen **(1)**
2. **(a)** carbon dioxide **(1)**
   (b) from the air **(1)** by diffusion **(1)** through the stomata in the leaf surface **(1)** *You need to mention the air, diffusion* ***and*** *stomata to get all the marks for this question.*
3. Photosynthesis can only take place in cells containing chloroplasts/chlorophyll. **(1)** Only some leaf cells contain these. **(1)**

21. Limiting factors

1. temperature, **(1)** light intensity, **(1)** carbon dioxide/CO_2 concentration **(1)**
2. a factor that limits the rate of photosynthesis **(1)** when it is at a low level **(1)**
3. Photosynthesis produces oxygen. **(1)** The more rapidly that oxygen is released, the faster the photosynthesis reactions must be happening. **(1)**

22. Water transport

1. **(a)** either water or mineral salts **(1)**
   (b) It was in the soil. **(1)**
2. xylem, **(1)** phloem **(1)**
3. **(a)** When water from inside a leaf turns to water vapour and diffuses out into the air. **(1)**
   (b) When water leaves the leaf by transpiration, it pulls water up the xylem through the plant. **(1)** This pulls water from the roots which causes water to move into the root from soil water. **(1)**

23. Osmosis

1. water **(1)** permeable **(1)**
2. net movement of water **(1)** from an area of high water concentration **(1)** to an area of low water concentration **(1)**
3. There is a higher concentration of water molecules on the right of the membrane than on the left. **(1)** Water molecules are small enough to pass through the partially permeable membrane so there will be osmosis from the right side to the left side of the membrane. **(1)** The volume on the left will increase as more water molecules cross the membrane, and volume on the right will fall. **(1)**

24. Organisms and the environment

1. a pooter **(1)**
2. to protect any organisms in the trap from sun and rain **(1)**
3. The organisms may not be evenly spread, **(1)** so averaging several results helps to even out random variation. **(1)**

25. Biology extended writing 3

Answers can be found on page 111.

26. Fossils and evolution

1. the history of life on Earth as shown by fossils **(1)** from different periods of time **(1)**
2. Any two from: fossils do not always form; soft tissue decays so some organisms don't make fossils; many fossils have not been found yet. **(1 each)**
3. Fossils show us what organisms looked like at different times in the past, **(1)** so they can show us how the organisms have changed over time, which is evolution. **(1)**

27. Growth

1. an increase in size, such as in length or mass **(1)**
2. **(a)** Any one from: measure its change in height over time; measure its change in mass over time; measure the change in number and size of leaves over time (or similar) **(1)** *The key point to include here is change over time.*
   (b) If the measurements increase over time, **(1)** then the plant is growing. **(1)**
3. A percentile chart shows the change in mass for different proportions of children/the population. **(1)** It can be used to check whether the rate of growth of a child is normal. **(1)**

28. Growth of plants and animals

1. Cell division is when a cell divides to make more cells. **(1)** Cell elongation is when cells grow longer. **(1)**
2. This is when cells develop into specialised cells such as muscle, nerve or brain cells. **(1)**
3. They are the cells in the plant or animal that can develop into any kind of specialised cell in the organism. **(1)**

29. Blood

1. oxygen in red blood cells **(1)** glucose in plasma **(1)**
2. Some white blood cells surround and destroy pathogens. **(1)** Other white blood cells produce antibodies that destroy pathogens. **(1)**

30. The heart

1. any one from: muscle tissue, nerve tissue, tendon tissue **(1)**
2. **(a)** They prevent the blood flowing the wrong way through the heart **(1)** when the heart muscles contract. **(1)**
   (b) Contraction of the left ventricle pumps blood all around the body, **(1)** which needs a bigger push than blood from the right ventricle, which is pumped just to the lungs. **(1)**

31. The circulatory system

1. heart **(1)** *This is the most likely answer, but blood vessels can also be considered as organs because they are formed from different tissues.*
2. It is an artery **(1)** because arteries are the blood vessels that carry blood away from the heart. **(1)**
3. to transport materials in the blood **(1)** around the body to where they are needed **(1)**

32. The digestive system

1. any two from: mouth; oesophagus; stomach; small intestine; large intestine; pancreas; liver **(2)** *There are other organs in the digestive system, but these are the only ones you are expected to know.*
2. small intestine **(1)**
3. The liver produces bile, which is released into the small intestine to help in the digestion of fats. **(1)** Food molecules absorbed from the small intestine into the blood are carried to the liver where they are processed/changed into other molecules. **(1)**

33. Breaking down food

1. proteases **(1)**
2. fatty acids **(1)** and glycerol **(1)**
3. amylase **(1)** *There are other examples but this is the one you are expected to know.*
4. to break down the large molecules in food **(1)** so that we can absorb them into our bodies **(1)**

34. Probiotics and prebiotics

1. any one from: probiotics; prebiotics; plant stanol esters **(1)**
2. They are supposed to encourage some kinds of bacteria in your digestive system. **(1)**
3. Either: Prebiotics **(1)** have been shown to reduce risk of diarrhoea and other health problems. **(1)**
   Or: Plant stanol esters **(1)** have been shown to reduce the level of cholesterol in the blood which should reduce the risk of heart disease. **(1)**

35 and 36. Biology extended writing 4 and 5

Answers can be found on page 111.

Chemistry answers

37. Structure of the atom

1. **(a)** protons, **(1)** neutrons **(1)**
   (b) protons, +1, **(1)** electrons, −1 **(1)**
2. atomic number = 9, **(1)** mass number = 19 **(1)**

38. The modern periodic table

1. **(a)** any one of: Na; K; Rb; Cs; Fr **(1)** *Remember that if the symbol for an element has two letters, the second one is always a lower case letter.*
   (b) any of: Be; B; C; N; O; F; Ne **(1)**
2. It is on the left hand side of the table **(1)** and all the metals are on the left. **(1)**
3. **(a)** K **(1)** **(b)** 39 **(1)**

39. Electron shells

1.

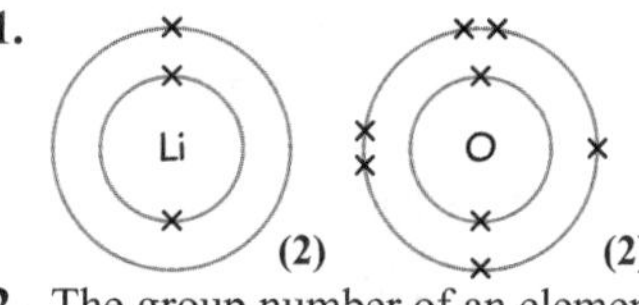

2. The group number of an element is the same as the number of outer electrons **(1)** so a sulfur atom has 6 outer electrons. **(1)**

40. Ions

1. **(a)** non-metals **(1)** **(b)** metals **(1)**
2. **(a)** Ca^{2+} **(1)** **(b)** F^- **(1)**

41. Ionic compounds

1. potassium hydroxide **(1)** because the name includes oxide **(1)**, copper carbonate and sodium sulfate **(1)** because the -ate means they contain oxygen **(1)**
2. **(a)** CaS **(1)** **(b)** $Mg(NO_3)_2$ **(1)** **(c)** K_2SO_4 **(1)**

42. Properties of ionic compounds

1. **(a)** conducts **(1)**
   (b) does not conduct **(1)**
   (c) conducts **(1)**
2. **(a)** insoluble **(1)** **(b)** soluble **(1)** **(c)** insoluble **(1)**

43. Precipitates

1. **(a)** A precipitate will form **(1)** of calcium carbonate **(1)** because calcium carbonate is insoluble. **(1)**
   (b) No precipitate will form **(1)** because both of the other combinations of ions are soluble. **(1)**

44. Ion tests

1. **(a)** calcium **(1)** **(b)** potassium **(1)**
2. **(a)** chloride **(1)**
   (b) carbonate **(1)** *The limewater is actually used to find out if a gas is carbon dioxide, but this is part of the test for carbonate ions.*
   (c) sulfate **(1)**

45. Chemistry extended writing 1

Answers can be found on page 111.

46. Covalent bonds

1. B **(1)**
2. **(a)** 4 **(1)**
   (b) A carbon atom shares one electron with each hydrogen atom **(1)** so it needs to share with four of them **(1)** to fill its outer shell. **(1)**

47. Covalent substances

1. It has a low melting point **(1)** because there are only weak forces between the different molecules. **(1)**
2. **(a)** All the atoms are held together by strong bonds. **(1)**
   (b) There are no charged particles. **(1)**
   (c) It has a high melting point **(1)** because the atoms are all held together by strong bonds. **(1)**

48. Miscible or immiscible?

1. **(a)** ethanol and water **(1)**
   (b) fractional **(1)** distillation **(1)**
2. Any two of the following points: Immiscible liquids will form two different layers **(1)** and if they were not mixed the person would only get some of the top layer on their salad. **(1)** Shaking the bottle mixes the two layers up temporarily. **(1)**

49. Chromatography

1. **(a)** D **(1)** **(b)** B **(1)** **(c)** C and E **(1)**
2. **(a)** $R_f = 4\,cm/10\,cm$ **(1)** = 0.4 **(1)**
   (b) The top spots for samples A, D and E **(1)**

50. Chemical classification 1

1. **(a)** simple molecular covalent substances **(1)** *If you put giant molecular covalent substances you were almost right – graphite is the only one of these substances that does conduct electricity.*
   (b) ionic substances and giant molecular covalent substances **(1)**
   (c) giant molecular covalent substances **(1)** *Ionic compounds are made of ions not atoms.*
2. Similarities: in both types of bonding the atoms end up with full outer electron shells. **(1)**
   Differences – any one from: in ionic bonding electrons are transferred to form ions but in covalent bonding the electrons are shared; **(1)** ionic bonding produces charged ions but covalent bonding produces neutral molecules **(1)**

51. Chemical classification 2

1. Metals conduct electricity when they are solids, **(1)** ionic substances only conduct electricity when they are molten or dissolved. **(1)**
2. **(a)** ionic or simple molecular covalent, **(1)** as some substances in both of these groups are soluble **(1)**
   (b) Either: Find out if the solution conducts electricity **(1)** as ionic substances conduct electricity when they are in solution (or simple molecular covalent substances do not conduct when they are in solution). **(1)**
   Or: Heat the substance **(1)** as ionic substances will not melt at temperatures that can be achieved in a school laboratory (or simple molecular covalent substances usually melt at temperatures that can be achieved). **(1)**

52. Metals and bonding

1. The metal ions are in a regular arrangement. **(1)** Some of the electrons from each atom can move between the ions. **(1)**
2. **(a)** Malleable means the metal can be hammered into shape without breaking. **(1)**
   (b) When a force is applied to a metal **(1)** the layers of ions can slide over each other fairly easily. **(1)**

53. Alkali metals

1. Any two points from: Rubidium is more reactive than potassium, **(1)** and so its reaction could be quite violent, **(1)** which would be dangerous. **(1)**
2. $2Na\ (s) + 2H_2O\ (l) \rightarrow 2NaOH\ (aq) + H_2\ (g)$ (**1** mark for correct substances, **1** for state symbols, **1** for balancing)

54. Halogens

1. The reaction with chlorine will be faster **(1)** because chlorine is more reactive than bromine (or because the halogens get more reactive as you go up the group). **(1)**
2. sodium + bromine → sodium bromide **(1)**
   $2Na + Br_2 \rightarrow 2NaBr$ (**1** mark for substances, **1** for balancing)

55. More halogen reactions

1. HCl(aq) (**1** for the formula, **1** for the state symbol) *Remember that hydrogen halides form acids when they dissolve in water.*
2. hydrogen + bromine → hydrogen bromide **(1)**
   $H_2(g) + Br_2(l) \rightarrow 2HBr(g)$ (**1** for correct reactants and products, **1** for balancing, **1** for state symbols) *Don't forget that the gases you need to know about for this course form molecules with two atoms, so the formula for hydrogen gas is H_2, not H.*

56. Noble gases

1. density: any answer between about 2.3 and 2.8; **(1)** and boiling point: any answer between about −130 and −100 **(1)**
2. **(a)** Helium has a low density **(1)** so it makes the airship float. **(1)**
   (b) Argon is inert **(1)** so it does not react with the hot metal. **(1)**

57 and 58. Chemistry extended writing 2 and 3

Answers can be found on page 111.

59. Temperature changes

1. It is an exothermic reaction **(1)** because combustion reactions release energy **(1)**.
2. **(a)** endothermic **(1)**
   (b) The energy taken in is greater than the energy released, **(1)** as this is why the temperature drops. **(1)**

60. Rates of reaction 1

1. **(a)** decrease, **(1)** **(b)** decrease, **(1)** **(c)** increase **(1)**

61. Rates of reaction 2

1. **(a)** unburnt fuel, **(1)** carbon monoxide, **(1)** oxygen **(1)**
   (b) carbon dioxide, **(1)** water **(1)**
2. Catalytic converters work best when they are hot. **(1)** The catalytic converter will be cold at the start of the journey **(1)** and may not convert all the carbon monoxide into carbon dioxide. **(1)**

62. Relative masses

1. **(a)** $CaO = 1 \times Ca + 1 \times O$
   $M_r = 40 + 16$ **(1)** $= 56$ **(1)**
   (b) $NH_3 = 1 \times N + 3 \times H$
   $M_r = 14 + (3 \times 1)$ **(1)**
   $= 17$ **(1)**
   (c) $CaCl_2 = 1 \times Ca + 2 \times Cl$
   $M_r = 40 + (2 \times 35.5)$ **(1)**
   $= 111$ **(1)**

63. Empirical formulae

1. Na: 8/23 = 0.348, O: 2.78/16 = 0.174 **(1)**
   Na: 0.348/0.174 = 2, O: 0.174/0.174 = 1 **(1)**
   Na_2O **(1)**

64. Percentage composition

1. 1 atom of carbon, A_r for C = 12
   $M_r = 12 + 4 = 16$ **(1)**
   percentage by mass = 1 × 12/16 × 100 **(1)**
   = 75% **(1)**
2. 2 atoms of carbon, A_r for C = 12
   $M_r = (2 \times 12) + (6 \times H) + 16 = 46$ **(1)** *Notice that there are hydrogen atoms at two different places in the formula.*
   percentage by mass = 2 × 12/46 × 100 **(1)**
   = 52% **(1)**

65. Yields

1. Theoretical yield is the amount of product that should be obtained worked out from the formula (or the amount obtained if the reaction is complete and nothing is spilled). **(1)** Actual yield is what is really obtained. **(1)**
2. percentage yield = 240 tonnes/600 tonnes **(1)**
   = 40% **(1)**

66. Waste and profit

1. **(a)** Any two from: people don't like living near landfill sites or incinerators; a landfill site or incinerator may cause house prices to drop; lorries transporting waste can cause dust or disturbance **(2)**
   (b) It costs the company money to transport the waste **(1)** and it may cost them money to make hazardous waste safe. **(1)**

67 and 68. Chemistry extended writing 4 and 5

Answers can be found on page 111.

Physics answers

69. Static electricity

1. **(a)** proton, neutron **(1)** **(b)** proton, neutron **(1)**
   (c) electron **(1)**
2. **(a)** Electrons have been transferred **(1)** from the comb to the cloth. **(1)** The comb now has fewer electrons than protons **(1)** so it has a positive charge. **(1)**
   (b) The comb will repel the rod (or the rod will move away) **(1)** because they both have the same charge (or because both charges are positive). **(1)**

70. Uses and dangers

1. You have built up a charge of static electricity, **(1)** which gives you a shock when it is earthed. **(1)**
2. Any one of: it can cause an explosion when aeroplanes are being refuelled; it can cause an explosion when fuel is being delivered to filling stations; lightning can kill living things. **(1)**
3. The paint is given a charge of static electricity. **(1)** The droplets spread out because they all have the same charge. **(1)** The object being painted is given the opposite charge **(1)** so the paint is attracted to it. **(1)**

71. Electric currents

1. electrons **(1)**
2. they always move in the same direction **(1)**

3. charge = 5 A × 20 s **(1)**
   = 100 C (**1** mark for 100, **1** for unit)

72. Current and voltage

1. ammeter **(1)**
2. **(a)**

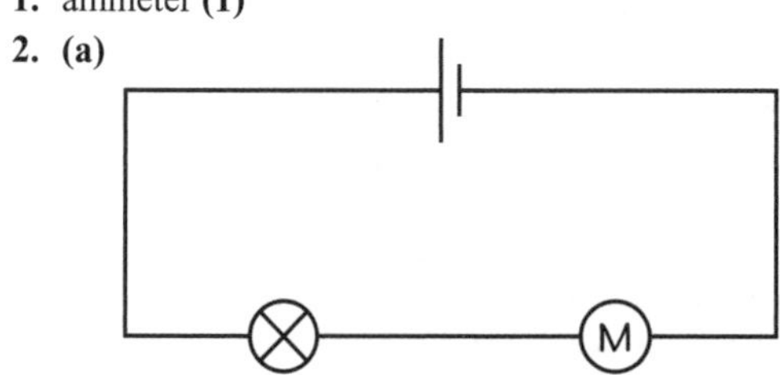

(**1** mark each for the correct symbols for the cell, bulb and motor, **1** mark for a drawing with no gaps in the circuit)

(b) **(1)**

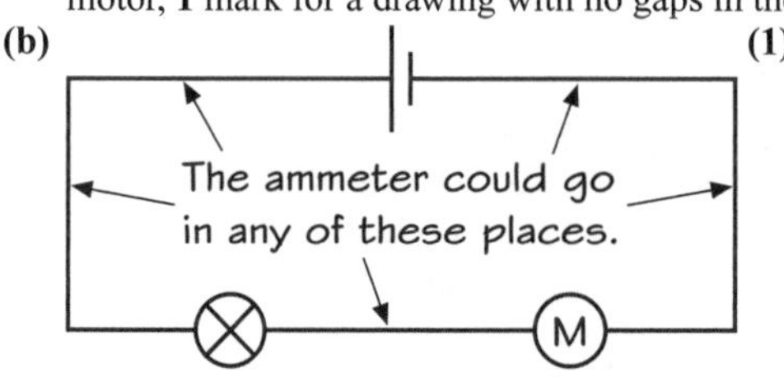

The ammeter could go in any of these places.
M

(c) voltmeter across the bulb, like this: **(1)**

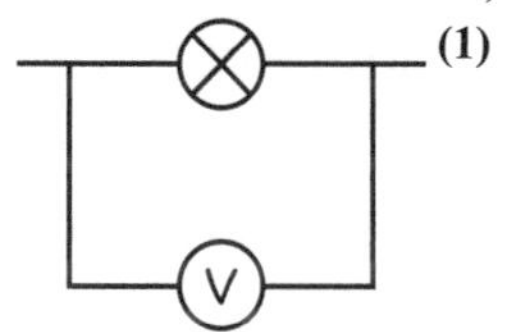

73. Resistance, current and voltage

1. **(a)** The current will go up. **(1)**
   (b) The current will go up. **(1)**
2. V = 2 A × 15 Ω **(1)**
   = 30 V (**1** for correct answer, **1** for correct units)
3. R = 6 V/2 A **(1)**
   = 3 Ω (**1** for correct answer, **1** for correct units)

74. Changing resistances

1. diode **(1)**
2. thermistor **(1)**
3. The resistance increases **(1)** as the filament gets hotter. **(1)**

75. Transferring energy

1. **(a)** watts **(1)**
   (b) joules **(1)**
2. P = 0.5 A × 6 V **(1)**
   = 3 W (**1** for correct answer, **1** for correct units)
3. 10 minutes = 600 seconds **(1)**
   E = 9 A × 230 V × 600 s **(1)**
   = 1 242 000 J (**1** for correct answer, **1** for correct units)

76. Physics extended writing 1

Answers can be found on page 111.

77. Vectors and velocity

1. Displacement has a size and a direction **(1)** but a distance only has a size. **(1)**
2. Distance = 80 m − 0 m = 80 m **(1)**
   Time = 60 − 0 = 60 s **(1)**
   Speed = 80 m/60 s **(1)**
   = 1.33 m/s **(1)**
   Remember to always show your working in calculation questions.

78. Velocity and acceleration

1. The train is stationary for 10 seconds, then it accelerates. It travels at a constant velocity of 20 m/s for 20 seconds and then it slows down for 20 seconds. Then it accelerates faster than before for 10 seconds, before travelling at a constant velocity of 40 m/s.
   (**3** marks if you got all of these points, **2** if you got most of them, **1** mark if you only got a few)
2. Initial velocity = 0 m/s, final velocity = 20 m/s,
   change in velocity = 20 − 0 = 20 m/s **(1)**
   Time taken = 20 s
   Acceleration = 20 m/s/20 s **(1)** = 1.0 m/s^2 **(1)**
3. Initial velocity = 20 m/s, final velocity = 10 m/s,
   change in velocity = 10 − 20 = −10 m/s **(1)**
   Time taken = 20 s
   Acceleration = −10 m/s/20 s **(1)** = −0.5 m/s^2 **(1)**
   Remember always to work out final velocity – initial velocity, then you will get the correct sign for the acceleration.

79. Resultant forces

1. **(a)** 100 N − 30 N **(1)** = 70 N **(1)**
   (b) The car will accelerate/its velocity will increase **(1)** because there is a forwards resultant force. **(1)**
2. **(a)** A diagram like the one for the boy standing on the floor, with labelled up and down arrows, **(1)** and both arrows the same size. **(1)**
   (b) Her weight pushing down on the chair **(1)** and the chair pushing up on her. **(1)**
   *For part **(a)**, think about the weight of the girl pulling the girl down, and the force from the chair pushing her up so that the forces are balanced. This is a free-body diagram, so both the forces are forces on the girl.*
   *For part **(b)**, think about the girl's weight pushing down on the chair, and the chair pushing back on her. This is an action and reaction diagram, so the two forces are on different objects.*
   Don't worry if you find this hard – most people find it difficult to explain the difference!

80. Forces and acceleration

1. Acceleration depends on force and mass. **(1)** If the mass is greater, it takes a larger force to give the same acceleration. **(1)**
2. F = 30 kg × 5 m/s^2 **(1)**
   = 150 N **(1)**
3. F = 1200 kg × 4 m/s^2 **(1)**
   = 4800 N. **(1)**

81. Terminal velocity

1. W = 62 kg × 10 N/kg **(1)**
   = 620 N **(1)**
2. Mass = 35/1000 kg = 0.035 kg **(1)**
   W = 0.035 kg × 10 N/kg **(1)**
   = 0.35 N **(1)**
3. **(a)** Acceleration is zero **(1)** because she is at terminal velocity/is not getting any faster. **(1)**
   (b) 700 N **(1)** because if she is at terminal velocity/not accelerating, her air resistance must be the same size as her weight. **(1)**

82. Stopping distances

1. **(a)** reaction time **(1)**
   (b) any one from: mass; brakes; road surface **(1)**
   (c) speed **(1)**
2. If the driver is tired her reactions will be slower **(1)** so the thinking distance will be longer (or she will travel further while she is reacting to the danger). **(1)** *Mention thinking distance or braking distance in answers, if you can.*

83. Momentum

1. The car has the biggest momentum **(1)** because it has the largest mass. **(1)**
2. momentum = 1200 kg × 15 m/s **(1)**
   = 18 000 kg m/s (**1** for answer, **1** for correct units)
3. Any three points from: The total momentum before and after a collision is the same (or momentum is conserved). **(1)** Momentum depends on velocity and mass. **(1)** The total mass of the car and van is greater than the mass of the van (or the mass of the moving objects has increased) **(1)** so the velocity must decrease. **(1)**

84. Momentum and safety

1. air bags, **(1)** seat belts, **(1)** crumple zones **(1)**

2. Any three from: They stop your head hitting the dashboard. **(1)** They are stretchy so you take a longer time to stop **(1)** than the rest of the car **(1)** so the forces on you are smaller. **(1)**
3. It takes longer for the main part of your body to stop if you bend your knees **(1)** so the rate of change of momentum is less **(1)** and the forces on you are smaller. **(1)**

85. Work and power

1. **(a)** work = 50 N × 1.5 m **(1)**
   = 75 J (**1** for correct answer, **1** for correct unit)
   (b) power = 75 J/2 s **(1)**
   = 37.5 W (**1** for correct answer, **1** for correct unit)
2. 10 minutes = 10 × 60 seconds = 600 seconds **(1)**
   power = 60 000 J/600 s **(1)**
   = 100 W **(1)**

86. Potential and kinetic energy

1. **(a)** GPE = 0.5 kg × 10 N/kg × 2 m **(1)**
   = 10 J (**1** for correct answer, **1** for unit)
   (b) 10 J **(1)**, as the gravitational potential energy it had on the shelf will all be converted to kinetic energy **(1)**
2. KE = $\frac{1}{2}$ × 45 kg × $(10\,\text{m/s})^2$ **(1)**
   = 2250 J (**1** for correct answer, **1** for unit)

87 and 88. Physics extended writing 2 and 3

Answers can be found on pages 111 and 112.

89. Isotopes

1. **(a)** 5 **(1)**
   (b) 11 **(1)** *The mass number is the total number of protons and neutrons.*
   (c) $^{11}_{5}\text{B}$ **(1)**
2. They both have 7 protons in the nucleus, **(1)** nitrogen-14 has 7 neutrons **(1)** and nitrogen-15 has 8 neutrons **(1)**
   You need to subtract the atomic number from the mass number to find the number of neutrons.

90. Ionising radiation

1. **(a)** Any two from: a helium nucleus; two protons and two neutrons; has a +2 charge (**1** mark for each point)
   (b) an electron, **(1)** with a −1 charge, **(1)**
2. **(a)** gamma radiation (or gamma rays) **(1)**
   (b) alpha radiation (or alpha particles) **(1)**

91. Nuclear reactions

1. radioactive decay, **(1)** fission, **(1)** fusion **(1)**
2. neutron **(1)**
3. A fission reaction releases neutrons. **(1)**
   Each neutron can make another nucleus split up, **(1)** which releases even more neutrons. **(1)**

92. Nuclear power

1. The heat is used to turn water to steam. **(1)** The steam makes a turbine spin **(1)** and the turbine drives a generator. **(1)**
2. **(a)** They control how fast the chain reaction happens. **(1)** If the control rods are put into the core the reaction slows down. **(1)** If they are pulled out the reaction speeds up. **(1)**
   (b) The moderator slows down the neutrons **(1)** produced by fission reactions **(1)** to make them more likely to cause another fission reaction. **(1)**

93. Fusion – our future?

1. Fission is a large nucleus splitting up. **(1)**
   Fusion is two small nuclei joining up. **(1)**
2. It needs to be published in a peer-reviewed journal, **(1)** and other scientists need to get the same results. **(1)**

94. Changing ideas

1. alpha particles, **(1)** beta particles, **(1)** gamma rays **(1)**
2. It may cause mutations in DNA, **(1)** which can damage cells and make them become cancerous. **(1)**
3. Use tongs to handle the source. **(1)** *Teachers do not normally wear overalls or breathing apparatus, although these are precautions that radiation workers could take.*

95. Nuclear waste

1. advantage – any one from: power stations do not produce carbon dioxide; supplies of nuclear fuel will last longer than supplies of fossil fuels **(1)** disadvantage – any one from: it is difficult and expensive to store nuclear waste; an accident could pollute a large area; people think it is dangerous **(1)**
2. An earthquake could damage the containers **(1)** and allow radioactive materials to escape. **(1)**

96. Half-life

1. the length of time it takes for half of the atoms in a sample to decay (or for the activity to become half its original value) **(1)**
2. Half of 60 is 30, half of 30 is 15, **(1)** so the 4 hours represents 2 half-lives. **(1)** The half life is 2 hours. **(1)**

97. Uses of radiation

1. **(a)** radon **(1)**
   (b) any three from: ground and buildings; medical; nuclear power; cosmic rays; food and drink (**1** mark each)
2. **(a)** Gamma rays are used to detect cancer by injecting a radioactive tracer into a patient; **(1)** a gamma camera detects where this collects **(1)** and this shows where there is more than usual cell activity. **(1)**
   (b) Gamma rays are targeted at cancers/tumours **(1)** to kill the cells. **(1)**

98. More uses of radiation

1. If the paper is too thin more beta particles get through **(1)** and the pressure on the rollers will be reduced. **(1)**
2. Four of the following points: An alpha source inside the smoke alarm ionises the air, **(1)** which allows a current to flow between two plates. **(1)** Smoke absorbs some of the alpha particles **(1)** so the current falls **(1)** and the alarm is sounded. **(1)**

99 and 100. Physics extended writing 4 and 5

Answers can be found on pages 111 and 112.

Extended writing answers

Below you will find a list of points which will help you to check how well you have answered each Extended writing question. Your actual answer should be written in complete sentences, it will contain lots of detail and will link the points into a logical order. A full answer will contain most of the points listed but does not have to include all of them and may include other valid statements. You are more likely to be awarded a higher mark if you use correct scientific language and are careful with your spelling and grammar.

15. Biology extended writing 1

Cell wall; made of cellulose; gives the cell support and helps it keep its shape; cytoplasm contains; water and dissolved salts; site for chemical reactions; which support cell process and life; vacuole; large space in the middle of the cell; filled with sap; helps keep cells rigid; chloroplasts; in the cytoplasm; contain chlorophyll; which absorbs light during photosynthesis; mitochondria; where respiration takes place; and so produce energy; cell membrane; keeps contents of cell from leaking out; controls movement of substances in and out of the cell; nucleus; contains DNA; controls the cell.

16. Biology extended writing 2

Enzymes have an active site; which is a fixed size/shape; so that it fits the substrate being broken down; if an enzyme is denatured; the size/shape of the active site changes; and it can no longer bind to the substrate; and break it down; temperature affects the activity of enzymes; enzymes like zymase will work best at an optimum temperature and very slowly at higher or lower temperatures; high temperatures cause enyzme molecule to change shape; and its active site is destroyed; low temperatures just slow down the reactions; pH affects the activity of enzymes; enzymes will have an optimum pH; lower or higher pH can cause denaturation; substrate concentration affects the activity of enzymes; if there is very little substrate, the reaction will also stop; if the substrate concentration rises too high then the rate at which the enzyme works hits a maximum level.

25. Biology extended writing 3

Photosynthesis makes glucose; from water and carbon dioxide; oxygen also produced; needs energy from sunlight to start the process; balanced chemical equation; surface cells of leaf are full of chloroplasts; which contain chlorophyll; chlorophyll traps sunlight; surface of leaf is waxy; to prevent water being lost; leaf full of air spaces; to allow gas exchange to take place; large surface area to volume ratio; underside of leaf has small holes; called stomata; open to allow carbon dioxide to diffuse in; and oxygen to diffuse out; whole leaf is thin; so that diffusion takes place over short distances.

35. Biology extended writing 4

Saliva; in the mouth; contains amylase; which is an enzyme; which starts to break down starch; into simple sugars; swallowing means that peristalsis takes food into the stomach; acid conditions; also helps break down starch molecules; pancreas; produces more amylase; to complete digestion of starch; to simple sugars; and then to glucose; in the small intestine; and absorbed; further down small intestine.

36. Biology extended writing 5

Heart; made of muscle; contains 4 chambers; pumps blood; pulmonary artery; takes deoxygenated blood; to lungs; pulmonary vein; brings oxygenated blood back; oxygenated blood pumped out through left ventricle/atrium; into aorta; and other arteries; carry oxygenated blood; away from the heart; capillaries; used to exchange oxygen and nutrients; with tissues/cells; veins; carry blood back to the heart; into the vena cava; and back into the right atrium/ventricle; valves; stop blood flowing backwards.

45. Chemistry extended writing 1

Calcium has electrons in 4 shells; so it is in period 4 of the periodic table; it has 2 electrons in its outer shell; so it is in group 2 of the periodic table; it is a metal; it will react by losing 2 electrons; to form 2+ ions.

Oxygen has electrons in 2 shells; so it is in period 2 of the periodic table; it has 6 electrons in its outer shell; so it is in group 6 of the periodic table; it is a non-metal; it will react with a metal (or it will react with calcium) by gaining two electrons; to form 2− ions.

When calcium and oxygen react together the oxygen gains the same number of electrons that calcium loses (or two electrons are transferred); so there is one calcium ion for every oxygen ion in calcium oxide; the formula is CaO.

57. Chemistry extended writing 2

Similarities: they are both coloured; they are both non-metals; they both have 7 electrons in their outer shell; they both gain one electron to form 1− ions; they both form covalent bonds with other non-metal elements; they both react with hydrogen to form a compound called a hydrogen halide; these compounds form acids when they are dissolved in water; they both react with metals to form metal halides.

You don't get any credit for saying that they are both in group 7, because the question tells you that.

Differences: fluorine is a gas at room temperature and bromine is a liquid (or fluorine has a lower boiling point than bromine); fluorine is pale yellow and bromine is red-brown; fluorine is more reactive than bromine; reactions of fluorine happen faster than reactions of bromine; bromine has more electron shells than fluorine; fluorine forms compounds called fluorides and bromine forms bromides; fluorine will displace bromine from solutions of its compounds but bromine cannot displace fluorine.

58. Chemistry extended writing 3

Similarities: they are both made from non-metal atoms; they both have covalent bonds holding atoms together; the bonds holding the atoms together are strong; neither substance will conduct electricity; they are both compounds containing two different elements; they both have two oxygen atoms for each atom of the other element in the compound.

Differences: silicon dioxide is a solid at room temperature and carbon dioxide is a gas; in silicon dioxide all the atoms are held together in one giant structure, but in carbon dioxide the atoms form separate, small molecules; in silicon dioxide all the forces between atoms are strong, but in carbon dioxide the forces between separate molecules are very weak; it takes a lot of heat energy to melt silicon dioxide; so it has a high melting point; it doesn't take much heat energy to melt or evaporate carbon dioxide because of the weak forces between molecules; so carbon dioxide has very low melting and boiling points.

67. Chemistry extended writing 4

Use the same volume of acid each time; use acid at the same temperature each time; use the same mass of magnesium each time; the magnesium must be in the same size pieces each time.

Find the mass of the flask, acid and cotton wool; do this with the magnesium on the balance outside the flask; drop the magnesium into the acid and put the cotton wool in; record the time it takes for the mass to stop changing; or, record the mass every 30 seconds; draw a graph to show how the mass changes with time; repeat with acids of at least two other concentrations.

The reaction should happen faster when the acid is more concentrated; the change in mass should be the same each time.

68. Chemistry extended writing 5

Yield is the mass of useful product formed in a reaction; the theoretical yield is the amount of product worked out using the equation; the actual yield is how much is obtained when the reaction is carried out; actual yield is less than the theoretical yield; because the reaction may stop before it is complete; this means some reactants are left over; some of the reactants or products may be lost when the reaction is carried out; such as liquids being spilled; or gases escaping; or products being left behind in a container; some of the reactants may react in different ways; to form different products.

76. Physics extended writing 1

Polythene rod: atoms normally have the same number of protons and electrons; so they have no overall charge; electrons are on the outside of.atoms; some electrons can be transferred by rubbing; protons cannot be moved because they are in the centre of atoms; when the polythene rod is rubbed some electrons are transferred from the cloth to the rod; so the rod has more electrons than protons; the cloth will have a positive charge; the rod will have a negative charge.

Acetate rod: rubbing will transfer electrons from the rod to the cloth; the rod will have fewer electrons than protons; so it will have a positive charge; the cloth will have extra electrons; so it will have a negative charge.

Picking up paper: the negative charge on the polythene rod will repel electrons in the paper; the electrons will move away from the surface; so the surface will have a positive charge; this is an induced charge; the positive charge will be attracted to the negative charge on the rod; so the rod can pick up the pieces of paper.

If you have answered by explaining how a charged acetate rod will pick up pieces of paper, you should have some of these points in your answer instead: the positive charge on the acetate rod will attract electrons in the paper; the electrons will move towards from the surface; so the surface will have a negative charge; this is an induced charge; the negative charge will be attracted to the positive charge on the rod; so the rod can pick up the pieces of paper.

87. Physics extended writing 2

On Earth: objects fall because they have weight; the force of gravity pulls them down; when an object first starts to fall its weight is the only force on it; it accelerates; as it gets faster its air resistance increases; so the resultant force on it is less; its acceleration is less; eventually its air resistance is the same size as its weight; so there is no resultant force; and it stops accelerating; it has now reached terminal velocity.

On the Moon: the force of the Moon's gravity pulls the object down; it accelerates downwards; there is no air to provide air resistance; so the (resultant) downward force stays the same; it continues to accelerate; until it hits the ground.

88. Physics extended writing 3

The electrical energy in the motor is converted to gravitational potential energy as the carriages move up the first rise; they have maximum GPE at the top; as they go down the other side they get faster; the GPE gets less as the carriages go down; the kinetic energy increases as they get faster; the GPE is being converted to KE; the GPE is least at the bottom of the slope; the KE is greatest at the bottom of the slope; the carriages slow down as they go up the next rise; the KE is being converted to GPE; the KE gets less as they go up; the GPE increases as they go up; the same transfers occur over each rise; there is also friction between the carriages and the track; friction will convert some kinetic energy to thermal/heat energy; which will spread out into the air; air resistance acts to slow down the carriages; air resistance will transfer some kinetic energy to thermal/ heat energy; by the time the carriages reach the end of the ridge most of the energy originally transferred to them by the electric motor; has spread out into the air as heat; so there is hardly any kinetic energy left; so the carriages are moving slowly at the end.

99. Physics extended writing 4

The top number on each symbol is the mass number (or nucleon number); it tells us the total number of protons and neutrons; in the nucleus of each atom; the bottom number is the atomic number (or proton number); it tells us the number of protons in each atom; it also tells us the number of electrons; as an atom has the same number of protons and electrons; it is the number of protons that determines which element an atom is.

The two carbon atoms are isotopes of carbon; they have the same number of protons; they have the same number of electrons; they have different numbers of neutrons; carbon-12 has 6 neutrons and carbon-14 has 8 neutrons; the nitrogen atom is different because it has 7 protons; but it is similar to carbon-14 because both elements have a mass number of 14.

100. Physics extended writing 5

They are all similar because they are all ionising radiations; they are all emitted by the nucleus of a radioactive atom; they are all emitted by a random process; alpha radiation and beta radiation are similar because they are both particles; they both have charges; gamma radiation is different because it is electromagnetic radiation; alpha particles consist of two protons and two neutrons; beta particles consist of an electron; alpha particles have more mass than beta particles; alpha particles have a +2 charge and beta particles have a –1 charge; they are all different because they have different penetration properties; gamma radiation is the most penetrating and alpha radiation is the least penetrating; they are all different because they have different ionising properties; alpha is the most ionising and gamma is the least ionising.

Published by Pearson Education Limited, a company incorporated in England and Wales, having its registered office at Edinburgh Gate, Harlow, Essex, CM20 2JE. Registered company number: 872828

www.pearsonschoolsandfecolleges.co.uk

Edited by Judith Head and Florence Production Ltd
Typeset by Tech-Set Ltd, Gateshead

First published 2012

16 15 14 13 12
10 9 8 7 6 5 4 3 2 1

British Library Cataloguing in Publication Data
A catalogue record for this book is available from the British Library

ISBN 978 1 446 90263 9

Printed in Slovakia by Neografia